ASCENDING H the EIGHTS

A Layman's Guide to
The Ladder of Divine Ascent

Father John Mack

Conciliar Press
Ben Lomond, California

Published by   Conciliar Press
                P.O. Box 76
                Ben Lomond, California 95005-0076

Printed in Canada

ISBN 1-888212-17-9

Quotations from *The Ladder of Divine Ascent* are taken from
the translation by Colm Luibheid and Norman Russell,
published by Paulist Press (Mahwah, NJ, 1982),
and are used by permission of the publisher.

Unless otherwise noted, all Scripture quotations are from
the New King James Version of the Bible, © 1982
by Thomas Nelson, Inc., Nashville, Tennessee
and are used by permission.

Library of Congress Cataloguing-in-Publication Data

Mack, John, Father
    Ascending the heights : a layman's guide to The ladder
    of divine ascent / John Mack.
        p. cm.
    ISBN 1-888212-17-9 (pbk.)
    1. John, Climacus, Saint 6th cent. Scala Paradisi. 2. Spiritual life—
      Orthodox Eastern Church. I. Title.
    BX382.J63 S335 2000
    248.4'814—dc21   00-026207

TABLE OF CONTENTS

FOREWORD

What a tragedy that the beginning of this third millennium since the Nativity in the flesh of the Lord Jesus Christ should find millions (if not billions) of men and women unwilling to uphold sound teaching, having itchy ears, turning away from truth and preferring, in its stead, fables (2 Tim. 4:3, 4). They vainly follow an ever-increasing number of dead-end paths, all of which at best will keep them earthbound, and at worst will make them hell-bound. They are either blind to or choose to ignore Him who is the only Way, the only Truth and the only Life (John 14:6). For nearly three millennia Christ-loving men and women have followed that Way, finding His yoke good and His burden light (Matt. 11:30), slowly but surely climbing the ladder of divine ascent, reaching its summit and thereby gaining access to His Father's house in which are many abodes (John 14:2), where they shall perpetually enjoy the delights which He has prepared for those who love Him (1 Cor. 2:9).

For this reason it gives me great joy to pen a few words commending to you this newest book by Father John Mack, "my son in the Lord, begotten to me in the Spirit," a most pious priest, a true Christ-lover and, therefore, one who, emboldened by God's call and promises and empowered by His grace, is making his way up that ladder of divine ascent. He humbly offers his words of counsel to us, not as an emotionally and spiritually distant pedagogue, but as a fellow climber. And he addresses them not only as an invitation to those who are contemplating beginning the climb, but, being a good shepherd and lover of all Christ's lambs, also as an encouragement to those who are on that precious and salvific ladder with him, be they on lower or higher rungs than he. May the Lord God remember his priesthood in His Kingdom always.

By the intercessions of the Most Holy Theotokos, who is the ladder by which the pre-eternal Logos came down from heaven, and those of our venerable and God-bearing Father John Climacus, who first defined the ladder by which we might ascend to heaven, may we all reach the highest rung of the ladder of divine ascent and be found worthy to enter into and abide throughout all ages in the Holy City, the New Jerusalem, the Bride and Wife of the Lamb (Rev. 21:9).

+BASIL
Titular Bishop of Enfeh al-Koura
Wichita, Kansas

INTRODUCTION TO
THE LADDER OF DIVINE ASCENT

In the sixth century, a monk living in the Egyptian desert by the name of John wrote a book outlining the spiritual life. In the centuries which have passed, this book, *The Ladder of Divine Ascent*, has become a mainstay of Orthodox spirituality. In fact, as Bishop KALLISTOS points out, "with the exception of the Bible and the service books, there is no work in Eastern Christianity that has been studied, copied and translated more often than *The Ladder of Divine Ascent*" (Paulist Press edition, p. 1).

For those who are unfamiliar with the *Ladder*, let me briefly summarize its structure and then explain my approach to it in this book. St. John based his entire book on the image of a ladder stretching from earth to heaven (see Gen. 28:12). His ladder has thirty rungs, one for each year of the hidden life of Christ. These thirty rungs, or steps, can be broken down into the following pattern:

I. The Break with the World: Renunciation, Detachment, Exile

II. The Practice of the Virtues (the Active Life)

A. The Fundamental Virtues: Obedience, Penitence, Remembrance of Death, Sorrow

B. The Struggle against the Passions

    1. Nonphysical Passions: Anger, Malice, Slander, Talkativeness, Falsehood, Deception

    2. Physical Passions: Gluttony, Lust, Avarice

    3. Nonphysical Passions: Insensitivity, Fear, Vainglory, Pride

III. Union with God (the Contemplative Life): Stillness, Prayer, Dispassion, Love

The Layman's Ladder

St. John's *Ladder* has been part of the formation of Orthodox monastics since it was first written. Even today, each Lent it is read in its entirety in Orthodox monasteries throughout the world. But we would be wrong to think that this book is only for monastics; it is not. It is equally important for nonmonastic Orthodox Christians to study its contents and to apply its teachings to their own lives.

Of course, this application has to be made wisely, taking into account the differences between the monastic and the nonmonastic settings. This is a key point. The spiritual way that monastics and nonmonastics follow is the same. To attain the heavenly kingdom, it is necessary for each Orthodox Christian to ascend the same rungs of the Ladder. But the way in which we live out our spirituality will differ according to our calling and our responsibilities.

The book that is in your hands is an attempt to help you understand how to apply *The Ladder of Divine Ascent* to life in a nonmonastic setting. Each chapter contains much that comes directly from St. John's writings (the quoted material appears in **boldface type**).* The rest of the material is my own commentary on St. John's words. This book, therefore, should be used as a primer to the *Ladder*.

I encourage you to read through this book, either in one sitting or over the course of several days and weeks. You might even want to make it a regular part of your Lenten discipline, reading one chapter each of the weekdays of Lent. Struggle with these teachings, and especially struggle with the "how" of applying them to your own life. If you wish, you may also read this book together with the complete *Ladder of Divine Ascent*. Think about my commentary and your own life, and then struggle with the full teaching of St. John as it relates to your own spiritual journey.

The End Is Joy

As we look at the *Ladder* in overview, we would do well to consider the following observation of St. John about the goal of our ascent to heaven:

A Christian is an imitator of Christ in thought, word and deed, as far as this is humanly possible, and he believes rightly and blamelessly in the Holy Trinity.

According to St. John, the goal of our life, which is the goal to which the *Ladder* will lead us, is Christocentric: to follow Christ, to become like God, to imitate and resemble Him in His divine love. This is dramatically demonstrated in the most famous icons of St. John Climacus. St. John is most often shown at the bottom of a ladder, pointing people up. Jesus is shown at the

---

* Quotations are taken from the translation by Colm Luibheid and Norman Russell, published by Paulist Press (Mahwah, NJ, 1982), and are used by permission of the publisher.

top of the ladder, with His arms outstretched ready to receive those who ascend. Demons are attacking those who are climbing the ladder, trying to pull them down to hell.

The message is clear: In order to ascend to heaven, it is necessary for us to fix our eyes on Jesus, the Author and Finisher of our faith. We will never make it to God if we fix our eyes on the method, on the rungs of the ladder. This will only lead us to despair, and/or a rigid legalism which will rob us of our joy. We must look to Jesus. We must keep our eyes on the Kingdom and view all of our struggles in its everlasting Light.

As Christians, we are not masochists. All of our spiritual struggles have as their goal the joy and true celebration of union with Christ. In a very real sense, we are the ultimate hedonists. We seek true and lasting joy—joy which will never end and joy which can never be taken away.

By God's grace, we have been enlightened, and so have come to understand that the joys of this world are fading and never last. This is why we subdue our body and reorient its direction. This is why we fast and pray. This is why we give alms. This is the reason for all of our ascetic labors: to remind our body that this world is passing away; to remind ourselves that true joy is only found in the everlasting Kingdom of our God and Savior Jesus Christ.

As St. John reminds us:

The man wearing blessed, God-given mourning like a wedding garment gets to know the spiritual laughter of the soul.

May God enable us, through the prayers of this Holy Father, to know the laughter of the soul!

STEP 1

TURNING OUR BACKS ON THE WORLD

St. John introduces us to the first step of the *Ladder of Divine Ascent* by issuing a serious reminder:

> **Of all created and rational beings, endowed with the dignity of free will, some are friends of God, some are His true servants, some are useless servants (cf. Luke 17:10), some are entirely estranged, and there are some who, for all their weakness, take their stand against Him.**

Of course, the question St. John intends to raise in our hearts is: "Which one am I?"

We know that not everyone who is baptized makes it successfully to heaven; not everyone who enters by the narrow door steadfastly walks the narrow path (see Matt. 7:13, 14). Baptism is no guarantee that we will ascend into heaven. A good beginning does not absolutely ensure a good ending! Indeed, the danger always exists that we may become **useless servants** who **think of**

1

11

themselves as having been worthy of the gift of baptism, but have not at all guarded their covenant with him.

This being the case, then, we must take seriously the direction and focus of our lives. As Jesus warns,

> *Not everyone who says to Me, "Lord, Lord," shall enter the kingdom of heaven, but he who does the will of My Father in heaven (Matt. 7:21).*

But how can we ascend to God? How do we begin? This is Step One. According to St. John, to begin our heaven-bound journey, we must purposely turn our backs on this world as our primary interest and concern.

Withdrawal from the world is a willing hatred of all that is materially prized, a denial of nature for the sake of what is above nature.

How easy it is for us to become obsessed with the things of this world! Even while claiming to be concerned for the Kingdom, we can be living fundamentally and principally for this world. St. John says that this is evidence of our **pleasure-loving disposition.** How often do we pamper this body of ours and live for earthly satisfaction and pleasure, while ignoring the concerns of the soul? This explains why we must embrace the **renunciation of life.** We must choose to place the importance of the soul above all else, and we must refuse to be diverted from this primary endeavor.

Of course, this makes sense and sounds good—it even sounds easy . . . until we actually try it. Then we learn that our bodies are opposed to taking second place. They do not like to be said "no" to. This is the result of the Fall. When Adam fell and disobeyed the commandment of God (when he broke the fast, as it were) he unleashed the body and reversed the natural order in man. Before sin, man's body was the servant of his soul. After the fall, the soul of man became subjected to his body.

To ascend to heaven, we must reverse the order within us. We must teach the body to assume its rightful position as the guardian and servant of the soul. This is why St. John insists:

> **Violence and unending pain are the lot of those who aim to ascend to heaven with the body, and this especially at the early stages of the enterprise, when our pleasure-loving disposition and our unfeeling hearts must travel through overwhelming grief toward the love of God and holiness. It is hard, truly hard. There has to be an abundance of invisible bitterness, especially for the careless, until our mind ... is brought through simplicity, deep freedom from anger and diligence to a love of holiness and guidance.**

Thank God, we do not have to do this alone. For Christ Himself stands ready to help us in our labors. This gives us sweetness in the midst of our bitter pains and joy in the context of sorrow. Once again, we must remember the goal of our struggle: it is heaven and the enjoyment of the presence of God for eternity. Without this motivation of love and *true* pleasure-seeking, we will not be able to endure the struggle. Many have fainted on the way because they lost sight of the destination.

> **Without such objectives the denial of the world makes no sense. God who judges the contest stands waiting to**

see how it ends for the one who has taken on this race.

Mistakenly, we sometimes succumb to the temptation of believing that the real life is found here below (on this earth), and that the more we ascend to God the further away we will be from "life." How opposite is the real situation!

An impious man is a rational being, one who must die, who runs away from life . . .

There is no life in this world and the things of this world. This is what Holy Scripture reminds us of:

Do not love the world or the things in the world. . . . [For] the world is passing away (1 John 2:15, 17).

When man fell, death entered into this world. Only by ascending to God will we find true life, for **God is the life of all free beings.** How hard it is to keep this perspective! How hard and how laborious at times to stand apart from our fellows who are insistent upon the absolute value of this life and this world, and to live for the eternal values of the Kingdom which will never die.

But God has supplied encouragement for us in this struggle as well. St. John puts it in a negative way:

Do not separate yourselves from the church assemblies.

In another place, he calls this **the royal way, the life of stillness** [inner peace] **shared with others.** This is why the Church, the community of the faithful, is so important for us in our journey toward heaven. Others who are struggling to renounce the world encourage and motivate us to renounce the world ourselves.

Individually we will fail. But together, as fellow seekers of heaven, we will succeed.

Woe the man living alone when he falls into despondency or sleepiness, carelessness or despair, for then he has no one among men to lift him up.

Who then is the wise and faithful Christian?

It is the man who has kept unquenched the warmth of his vocation, who adds fire each day to fire, fervor to fervor, zeal to zeal, love to love, and this to the end of his life.

This is the first step. Let him who has set foot on it never turn back.

STEP 2

HOLDING ALL THINGS WITH OPEN HANDS

St. John introduces the second step of the Ladder to heaven with these provocative words:

> If you truly love God and long to reach the kingdom that is to come, if you are truly pained by your failings and are mindful of punishment and of the eternal judgment, if you are truly afraid to die, then it will not be possible to have an attachment, or anxiety, or concern for money, for possessions, for family relationships, for worldly glory, for love and brotherhood, indeed for anything of earth. All worry about one's condition, even for one's body, will be pushed aside as hateful. Stripped of all thoughts of these, caring nothing about them, one will turn freely to Christ.

2

This lack of concern for the things belonging to this world St. John calls **detachment**. For those called to the monastic life, this detachment is total: a monk leaves his family, his possessions, everything he owns and holds dear in order to embrace the Kingdom.

For those who are called to live in the world, the way of detachment is externally less severe. We live out our faith in the context of family, possessions, and "things." Living in the world necessitates a certain external attachment to the things of this world. But, although this way seems to be easier, in reality to live in the world is much more difficult. Temptations to become attached to "things" abound. We are surrounded by a superabundance of "things." We work hard to attain "things." We must learn how to practice detachment of the heart.

St. John says that there are three areas in which we must practice the virtue of detachment. We must detach ourselves:

- from worldly concerns;
- from selfishness;
- from the vanity that follows obedience.

For those who of us who live in the world, it is the last two which especially concern us.

We must hold all of the things of this world with open hands. We must be willing to part with them whenever we are asked for them. If we find in our hearts an unwillingness to part with anything (because we love it), there is improper attachment. If we find ourselves becoming angry because others have taken or misused our things, then there is improper attachment. If we find ourselves becoming jealous or envious of others because of the things which they possess, then there is improper attachment. In short, whenever we want or do anything just to bring pleasure to ourselves, there is improper attachment.

In addition to this detachment from selfish possessiveness, we must also be very careful not to become addicted to the praise of men. St. John describes it in this way:

I have seen many different plants of the virtues planted by them in the world, watered by vanity as if from an underground cesspool, made to shoot up by love of show, manured by praise.

This is the sin of the Pharisees: to love the praise of men; to become attached to the opinions of others. There is a wonderful story in the life of St. Macarius the Great which illustrates this point.

St. Macarius was once asked by a pilgrim how to find salvation in the world. He told the man to go to the cemetery and insult the dead people who were buried there. This he did and then returned to the saint. The saint then told him to return to the cemetery and sing the praises of those who were buried there. This he did and returned.

The saint then asked the pilgrim: "What did the dead people do when you insulted them?"

"Why, nothing, of course, Holy Father," the man replied.

St. Macarius continued, "What did the dead people do when you praised them?"

"Why, nothing, of course, Holy Father," the man replied again.

"Go and do the same, and you will be saved. Be dead

both to the praises and the curses of men and you will obtain salvation."

How truly hard this counsel is—yet how necessary and how freeing. To be free from concern for things and for the opinions of others is a great gift. In the words of St. John, it is to be **cleansed of grief.**

This is the second step, and if you take it, then do as Lot did, not his wife, and flee.

STEP 3

LIVING AS STRANGERS

The third step on our ascent to God is labeled by St. John as **Exile.** He defines it in this way:

> **Exile is a separation from everything, in order that one may hold on totally to God. . . . An exile is a fugitive, running from all relationships with his own relatives and with strangers.**

These words, which are indeed strong, are not only for monastics. It would certainly make our lives in the world a lot easier if we could simply dismiss this as advice only for monks and nuns. But it also would make our lives more empty of God! St. John Climacus' words remind us of St. Peter's description of every Christian:

> *Beloved, I beg you as* sojourners and pilgrims, *abstain from fleshly lusts which war against the soul (1 Pet. 2:11, emphasis added).*

3

And they also seem mild compared to the instruction of our Lord:

> *He who loves father or mother more than Me is not worthy of*
> *Me. And he who loves son or daughter more than Me is not*
> *worthy of Me (Matt. 10:37, 38).*

Family relationships are good things, ordained and established by God. So too are our friendships and the deep love which comes from them. Marriage is an honorable estate, ordained and sanctified by God. However, even good things can get in the way of our ascent to God. The great danger is that we will allow our relationships to keep us from pursuing God.

This is most obviously true about relationships with people who are not pursuing God at all. St. Paul reminds us:

> *Do not be deceived: "Evil company corrupts good habits"*
> *(1 Cor. 15:33).*

It is better to remain alone than to be attached intimately to and with someone who does not share our desire for God or our understanding of the Orthodox Faith.

To follow hard after God means that we must often endure the offenses and insults of those around us who do not understand our desire to find God and to experience Him in our lives. To practice exile means that we choose God rather than them. We are encouraged by the example of Moses:

> *By faith Moses, when he became of age, refused to be called the*
> *son of Pharaoh's daughter, choosing rather to suffer affliction*
> *with the people of God than to enjoy the passing pleasures of*
> *sin (Heb. 11:24, 25).*

As Christians we do not belong to this world; Jesus reminds us that we are *not of this world* (John 15:19). *In* the world, yes; but *of* it, never! Therefore, we will often feel like strangers, those who do not fit into the rhythms and patterns of this world. This is exile—to accept and rejoice in the loneliness of the Christian's life in the world.

Of course, it becomes much more difficult to discern how the virtue of exile applies to our relationships with fellow Orthodox Christians. These relationships are good, and our tradition insists that they must not be neglected in the formation of our own spiritual lives. We need each other; together we find salvation.

However, there is a danger even in good relationships. These relationships can sometimes take the place of God in our lives. We can begin to look to people (even good people) to be God for us. We can substitute relationships with spiritual people for a relationship with God. Exile reminds us of this danger.

Especially during Lent, when we are encouraged to practice silence and solitude, it is good to reorient ourselves toward God alone. Not that we stop pursuing our healthy and positive relationships, but rather that we determine in our hearts and minds that these relationships are important to us, not because of how they make us feel, but rather because of how they help us pursue God. As St. John writes:

> **Let your father be the one who is able and willing to labor with you in bearing the burden of your sins, and your mother the compunction that is strong enough to wash away your filth. Let your brother be your companion and rival in the race that leads to heaven, and may the constant thought of death be your spouse. Let your**

longed-for offspring be the moanings of your heart. May your body be your slave, and your friends the holy powers who can help you at the hour of dying if they become your friends.

This is the third step, equaling the number of the Three Persons. Whoever has reached it should look neither to right nor left.

STEP 4

PRACTICING OBEDIENCE

St. John Climacus labels the fourth rung on the Ladder to heaven **Obedience.** What is obedience? He describes it thus:

> . . . **a total renunciation of our own life, and it shows up clearly in the way we act. Obedience is the burial place of the will. . . . Obedience is self-mistrust up to one's dying day, in every matter, even the good.**

St. John is very insistent that without obedience no one will attain heaven. But his emphasis in this regard is very Orthodox. We do not obey so that we may fulfill some external set of rules and thus earn God's favor and love. This kind of thinking is very foreign to St. John.

Our obedience does not earn us anything. Rather, the act of obedience changes us and makes us ready to receive the love which God has already given to mankind in Christ. It was disobedience which lost Paradise for mankind. It is obedience which will regain it. As St. John writes:

> **Humility arises out of obedience, and from humility it-self comes dispassion, for "the Lord remembered us in our humility and saved us from our enemies."**

Obedience is necessary because to obey is to cut off our self-will and pride. To obey is to learn not to judge. To obey is to practice patience.

St. John Climacus records for us one of his discussions with a saint. The saint said to St. John:

> **Wise man, if you have consciously within you the power of him who said, "I can do everything in Christ who strengthens me," if the Holy Spirit has come upon you as on the Holy Virgin with the dew of purity, if the power of the Most High has cast the shadow of patience over you, then, like Christ our God, gird your loins with the towel of obedience, rise from the supper of stillness, wash the feet of your brethren in a spirit of contrition, and roll yourself under the feet of the brethren with humbled will.... Shed your will as if it were some dis-graceful garment.**

It is our own stubborn self-will which will keep us out of heaven. It is demanding that things be done our way on our own time schedule which destroys us spiritually. Obedience is the cure for this disease. Obedience is a way for us to cut off our own will and thus achieve sanctity.

A story from the *Institutes* of St. John Cassian confirms this teaching.

St. John Cassian once went to see an old man who was known to be perfect and a great wonder-worker. When he asked the old man to describe his road to sanctity, the elder replied: "I have never done anything of my own will and I have never taught anyone to do something which I do not do myself."

Undoubtedly, in the monastic environment in which St. John is writing, the obedience of which he speaks is very strict and exacting. A disciple is to give his spiritual father unquestioning obedience and to entrust his entire life into the hands of his "abba." As many spiritual fathers have noted, this kind of unquestioning obedience is unique to the monastic life, both because it is rendered in fulfillment of a vow, and because it is appropriate only to settings in which there are true spiritual elders who have attained heights of spiritual maturity.

How then can those living in the world, not surrounded by perfect elders, ascend to heaven through the practice of obedience? Let me humbly suggest a few ideas.

(1) Obey those in authority.

We should cheerfully obey, without question or disagreement, the instructions given to us by those in authority over us at work, home, church, and school. Here of course, we are not talking about spiritual direction, but about doing what we are told to, when we are told to do it, in the way that we are told to do it. Each command gives us an opportunity to cut off our own will, to humble ourselves, to refrain from argument and judgment, to abandon our own thoughts, and to fulfill cheerfully the instructions of another. How much positive spiritual growth can occur in one day's worth of obedience!

(2) Obey your father confessor.

We can make frequent use of the sacrament of confession and ask for advice and counsel on the direction of our spiritual lives. There are many decisions we make by ourselves that we should make in consultation with our father confessor. Remember the saying of the Fathers: "He who has himself for his spiritual father has for his spiritual father a fool!" How much better and safer it would be for us if we checked things out with our confessor before we set out on our own way. Not that we can look to him as we would to a clairvoyant elder; but we can and should look to him as a trusted guide, with whom we can be honest and from whom we can receive direction.

(3) Submit to your friends and family members.

We can begin to look for ways to obey in the relationships of life. We are all familiar with the saying, "Your wish is my command." What if we began to look at our closest family members and friends with this attitude? How much cutting off of our own will, how much patience, how much obedience we would learn if we became proactive in the fulfilling of the needs and desires of others. Is someone thirsty? Why don't you get up and get him something to drink? Is she hungry? Fix her something to eat. Does he need a book from the library? Offer to get it for him. Does she need a ride? Give it to her.

There is a wealth of spiritual opportunities awaiting us in every relationship if we see obedience as the goal. What if we stopped insisting on the correctness of our own way? It is an evidence of pride to think that we know best how and what to do. Why don't we obey the suggestions of our friends and spouses? Even if we are right, does it really make a difference which road we take to get there? Does it really matter how we put it together? So what if it takes more time? Is the spiritual danger of being proved right worth the stress of insisting on our own way? And aren't the spiritual advantages of obedience more important than time and money?

(4) Emulate the saints.

We can set before ourselves the lives and examples of the saints and seek to emulate their lives as much as we are able. Obedience is not the fulfillment of an abstract set of rules, but conformity to a person. The person after whom we are to pattern our entire life is our Lord and Savior Jesus Christ. How do we conform our lives to His? What does this mean? How do we express our obedience to Him in the ins and outs of life? The answer is found in the lives of the saints. From them and from the varied examples of their lives, we can learn how to obey Him who is the source and foundation of our lives.

(5) Seek the advice of trusted friends.

We can discuss our lives with friends whom we trust. Fr. Seraphim Rose used to talk about the need for "spiritual brothers" in our day and age, which is almost devoid of true spiritual fathers. Before we do things, before we set out on our own way doing our own things, we should always talk to people we respect *first!* And we should ask their blessing. I know this may seem silly, but there is a monastic story which confirms the practice.

> An elder at the end of his life was unable to keep the fast strictly (that is, to take no food or drink before the ninth hour) because of his poor health, but he would not eat without a blessing. A time came when all the monastic

fathers were away, and the only one to ask was a little boy.
He asked the boy: "Son, may I eat?"

The boy replied, "Eat, father!"

This happened three times. The last time the boy said,
"What kind of a monk are you? All you ever think about
is eating!"

The saint would not break his fast without a blessing. He was
so afraid of deceiving himself that he willingly chose to be hu-
miliated in the eyes of a little child. Would to God that we were
so afraid of self-deception. Would to God that we were so zeal-
ous for attaining the virtue of obedience.

**This step is of equal number with the evangelists. Keep
running, athlete, and do not be afraid.**

STEP 5

TURNING OUR BACKS ON SIN

Once John outran Peter, and now obedience is placed before repentance. For the one who arrived first represents obedience, the other repentance.

With these words, St. John Climacus introduces us to Rung Five of the Ladder which leads us to heaven. His definition of repentance is striking:

Repentance is the renewal of baptism and is a contract with God for a fresh start in life. Repentance goes shopping for humility and is ever distrustful of bodily comfort. Repentance is critical awareness and a sure watch over oneself. Repentance is the daughter of hope and the refusal to despair. (The penitent stands guilty—but undisgraced.) Repentance is reconciliation with the Lord by the performance of good deeds

5

**which are the opposites of the sins. It is the purifica-
tion of conscience and the voluntary endurance of af-
fliction. The penitent deals out his own punishment,
for repentance is the fierce persecution of the stomach
and the flogging of the soul into intense awareness.**

A friend of mine some time ago asked an experienced
monastic for a word of instruction. The monk looked at him
and said:

You spend too much time trying to do everything right.
You try too hard to be successful. This is your problem.
You are not good enough to make it to heaven on the
basis of your good deeds, but you don't repent enough to
make it on the basis of your sorrow. Try harder to repent
and you shall be saved.

The spirit of this monastic advice is in keeping with the words
of St. John. Not that we shouldn't try hard to do things right, but
we should realize at all times and in all things that we are, to use
the words of Jesus, but unprofitable servants.

We should indeed try harder to repent than to do anything
else. We should be more concerned with finding our faults than
we are with noticing our accomplishments. We should sorrow
more for our failures than we rejoice in our successes. We should
blame ourselves more readily than others. We should accept the
rebukes of others as just and worthy. And we should accept the
disappointments and difficulties of life without complaint. For as
St. John notes:

**A proof of our having been delivered from our failings
is the unceasing acknowledging of our indebtedness.**

... A sign of true repentance is the admission that all our troubles, and more besides, whether visible or not, were richly deserved.

Without repentance no one will ascend the Ladder to heaven. This is why Satan works so hard at keeping us from true repentance. His methods are diverse.

God is merciful before a fall, inexorable after—so the demons say. And when you have sinned, pay no attention to him who says in regard to minor failings: "If only you had not committed that major fault! This is nothing by comparison." The truth is that very often small gifts soften the great anger of the Judge.

He who really keeps track of what he has done will consider as lost every day during which he did not mourn, regardless of whatever good he may happen to have done. ... We ought to be on our guard, in case our conscience has stopped troubling us, not so much because of its being clear but because of its being immersed in sin.

In contemporary American Orthodoxy, how important this reminder is! The way to God is hard, and not every one that enters the race will receive the prize. Yes, God is loving and desires that all will be saved and come to the knowledge of the truth. But not all are willing to endure the suffering and pain that come from embracing the truth about themselves. Only the humble and the penitent can be saved, because only the humble and penitent are willing to embrace despair of themselves. And it is only despair of self which leads to true faith in the Infinite Other, who alone can save.

We must be very careful as Orthodox Christians not to fall into the heresy of Origen, who taught that all will be saved. St. John's words are addressed to us:

All of us . . . should be especially careful not to be afflicted with the disease of the godless Origen. This foul disease uses God's love for man as an excuse and is very welcome to those who are lovers of pleasure.

Sin is serious! To offend the living and loving God is monstrous evil. To turn away from His compassion and to follow our own way is the height of rebellion and the greatest offense. Let us be done with playing around with sin. Let us be done with downplaying the significance of our offenses. Even the littlest offense is worthy of eternal hellfire!

Let us bow low before God and beg of Him the forgiveness of our sins. Let us beseech Him to remove far from us coldness of heart and insensitivity to offense. Let us stop pretending that we are holy when we are empty of true sanctity. Let us be honest with God and with ourselves. *And let us repent!*

Through repentance you have reached the fifth step. You have, in this way, purified the five senses, and by choosing to accept punishment have thereby avoided the punishment that is involuntary.

STEP 6

REMEMBERING OUR MORTALITY

Each day, in our morning and evening prayers, as we pray for the repose of our departed loved ones, we are introduced to the theme of St. John's sixth step: **The Remembrance of Death.** St. John has powerful things to say about this:

> **Just as bread is the most necessary of all foods, so the thought of death is the most essential of all works....**
>
> **The man who lives daily with the thought of death is to be admired, and the man who gives himself to it by the hour is surely a saint.**

The remembrance of death—a sure and constant remembrance that I must die, that my death may come at any time, and that after death I must give an account for how I have lived this life—is a powerful incitement to godly living. St. John records the story of Hesychius the Horebite for our edification:

6

All his life he was careless and he paid not the slightest attention to his soul. Then a very grievous illness came on him, so that he was for a whole hour absent from the body. After he had revived, he begged us all to go away at once, built up the door of his cell, and remained twelve years inside without ever speaking to anyone and taking only bread and water. He never stirred and was always intent on what it was he had seen in his ecstasy. He never moved and had the look of someone who was out of his mind. And, silently, he wept warm tears. But when he was on the point of death, we broke in and asked him many questions. All he would say was this: "Please forgive me. No one who has acquired the remembrance of death will ever be able to sin."

As we think about those who have gone before us, let us always remember that very soon we shall join them in the grave. Death comes to all, and to many it comes early. In the grave, all the distinctions between men are obliterated. Where is the strong and where is the weak? Where is the rich and where is the poor? Where is the beautiful and where is the ugly? Where is the Ph.D. and where is the high-school dropout? Do they not all look the same as they decay in their graves? Will we not join them?

This life is very short. Why then do we spend so much time trying to make this short, passing life comfortable and happy? Why do we not spend more time preparing for the life which will follow? That life is eternal. That life will never end. And either we will enjoy Paradise because of how we labored here, or we will endure the fires of hell because of how we did not labor here.

We often live as if we will never die. We act as if we are

immortal and there will always be time enough for God later. This is monstrously stupid! Let us embrace true wisdom. Let us remember our death, and in remembering our death, let us repent of our preoccupation with this world.

> **Someone has said that you cannot pass a day devoutly unless you think of it as your last. . . . This, then, is the sixth step. He who has climbed it will never sin. "Remember your last end, and you will never sin" (Ecclus. 7:36).**

STEP 7

BEING REALISTIC ABOUT LIFE

So far, we have examined six rungs: **Renunciation, Detachment, Exile, Obedience, Repentance,** and **Remembrance of Death.** Now we are ready to look at the seventh: **Mourning.** St. John describes it this way:

> Mourning which is according to God is a melancholy of the soul, a disposition of an anguished heart that passionately seeks what it thirsts for, and when it fails to attain it, pursues it diligently and follows behind it lamenting bitterly.

As a step on the Ladder, mourning yields abundant results:

> Those who make some progress in blessed mourning are usually temperate and untalkative. Those who have succeeded in making real progress do not become angry and do not bear grudges. As for the perfect—these are humble,

7

they long for dishonor, they look out for involuntary sufferings, they do not condemn sinners and they are inordinately compassionate.

What exactly does St. John mean by mourning, and how can we begin to mourn? Obviously he means something different from simply mourning over our sin, because he has already listed the step of repentance. To mourn in this context is not to repent, although repentance is part of the mourning process.

To mourn is to embrace a sober view of life which takes into account the reality of human suffering (all a result of sin, which is how repentance and mourning are related), the shortness of human life (which is why remembrance of death leads to mourning), and the exactitude of divine judgment. It is to see ourselves as finite creatures who are caught up in a large web of sickening violence, exploitation, and abuse. It is to see the entirety of humanity as tragically deceived by the devil. It is to weep over the state of mankind and our involvement in and contribution to that tragedy.

To mourn is to echo the words of the Jews living in a foreign land who were asked to sing songs of joy:

> *How shall we sing the Lord's song*
> *In a foreign land?*
> *If I forget you, O Jerusalem,*
> *Let my right hand forget its skill!*
> *If I do not remember you,*
> *Let my tongue cling to the roof of my mouth (Ps. 137:6).*

To mourn is to abandon a pleasure-oriented way of life. To mourn is to stop living for fun. To mourn is to realize that my life is intertwined with all of humanity, and that I cannot live in isolation from the suffering masses. Listen to St. John's advice:

> **Think of your lying in bed as an image of the lying in your grave; then you will not sleep so much. When you eat at table, remember the food of worms; then you will not live so highly. When you drink water, remember the thirst of the flames; then you will certainly do violence to your nature. . . . Let the thought of eternal fire lie down with you in the evening and get up with you in the morning. Then indolence will never overwhelm you when it is time to sing the psalms.**

St. John also tells the story of a solitary named Stephen to remind us of the importance of everything we are talking about. This story, if taken into our souls, will teach us how to mourn:

> **A man called Stephen once lived here as a solitary. He spent many years in the wrestling-school of monastic life. Tears and fasting adorned his soul, as did many other fine achievements. His cell was on the side of the sacred mountain where the holy prophet and seer of God Elijah had once lived. He became famous and later he decided to practice a vastly more effective, ascetic and strict life of penance, and so moved on to Siddim, an abode of hermits. He spent several years there and lived very strictly. It was a place lacking every comfort and was rarely visited. . . .**
> **Near the end of his life, the old man returned to the holy mountain [Sinai]. . . . After a few days he was stricken by the illness from which he would eventually**

die. On the day before his death, he went into ecstasy and began to look to the right and to the left of his bed. He seemed to be rendering an account to someone, and in the hearing of the bystanders he said: "Of course it is true. That was why I fasted for so many years." Or again: "Yes, that is correct, but I wept and served my brothers." Or again: "No. You are accusing me falsely." Or sometimes: "Quite right. No, I have no excuse. But God is merciful."

This unseen and relentless interrogation was a truly awful and frightening spectacle. Worst of all was the fact that he was charged with offenses of which he was innocent, and, what is extraordinary, regarding some of them this hesychast and hermit would say, "I do not know how to answer." And yet he had been a monk for almost forty years and he had the gift of tears as well. Alas, alas! . . . He was truly unable to say such a thing. And why was that? Glory to Him who alone knows, and this was a man who had reared a leopard by hand in the desert, or so I was solemnly told. So there he was now, called to account, and he died while it was happening leaving us unsure of the judgment passed on him, of his final end or sentence or of the verdict rendered him.

If these words do not convict us, then this certainly will:

When we die, we will not be criticized for having failed to work miracles. We will not be accused of having failed to be theologians or contemplatives. But we will certainly have some explanation to offer to God for not having mourned unceasingly.

Such, then, is the seventh step. May he who has been found worthy of it help me too. He himself has already been helped, for by taking this seventh step he has washed away the stains of the world.

STEP 8

BENDING WITHOUT BREAKING

We are ready to turn our attention to Step Eight of the Ladder to heaven. St. John labels it **On Meekness** and introduces it this way:

> **As the gradual pouring of water on a fire puts out the flame completely, so the tears of genuine mourning can extinguish every flame of anger and irascibility.**

When we looked at **Mourning** we noted that St. John is describing a life of sobriety. To mourn is to realize that we are all caught in a large web of sin and deceit; it is to recognize and fully believe that perfection is not possible in this world (even the saints made mistakes!); it is to pursue only that Kingdom which is to come. Those who have grasped what St. John is describing can understand why the next step is to put aside anger.

Why do we become angry? Is it not most often because we are pursuing the perfect in this world? Is it not because we are busy building up our own "kingdoms" instead of the Kingdom of God? Is it not because we are concerned about how we appear and are treated in this world, rather than how we will appear and be treated in the world to come? Does not our anger most often have its source in our exalted opinions of the possibilities and capabilities of ourselves and of all those who are around us?

Anger is a terrible passion which drives away from us the Spirit of God and allows the demonic spirits to inhabit our souls. Anger, when it is given license in our souls, distorts our perspective, muddles our thinking, confuses our heart, and renders us unable to defend ourselves against the attacks of Satan. St. John describes it this way:

Angry people, because of their self-esteem, make a pitiable sight, though they do not realize this themselves. They get angry and then, when thwarted, they become furious.

Meekness is the antidote to anger.

So, then, anger the oppressor must be restrained by the chains of meekness, beaten by patience, hauled away by blessed love.

St. John is very practical in his advice for developing meekness. Meekness is first of all developed by not answering back when we are spoken to in an angry way. Those who are beginning on the road to meekness must take as their first rule: *I will never speak in an angry tone of voice to anyone who speaks in anger to me. I will not answer back in kind.* They should then extend this rule to include the following: *I will never allow myself to speak in anger to anyone,* period. This is especially true when I give advice or counsel or rebuke to those who are under my authority.

Those who are progressing on the road to meekness must take as their second rule: *I will not allow my mind to think angry thoughts against those who speak in angry words to me.* By extension, this means: *I will not allow my mind to think angry thoughts against anyone,* period. *I will not cherish thoughts of revenge or harbor ill feelings against anyone.* Those who have progressed this far are close to perfection: *I will not notice those who offend me.*

These have achieved true inner peace. The goal of meekness is not merely to say nothing back, nor is it to think nothing—it is to notice nothing; to be so absent from self-concern and others-concern that the praise and the rebukes of men are not even noticed! Can you even begin to imagine the joy and the inner freedom of those who have attained this position? The tyranny of the opinions of others, the ability of others to control our lives by "making us angry" through their treatment of us, is terrible bondage. To be freed from this is wonderful freedom. The road to this freedom is before us:

Take [anger] before the tribunal of reason and have it examined in the following terms: "Wretch, tell us the name of your father, the name of the mother who bore you to bring calamity into the world, the names of your loathsome sons and daughters. Tell us, also, who your enemies are and who has the power to kill you." And this is how anger replies: "I come from many sources and I have more than one father. My mothers are Vainglory, Avarice, Greed. And Lust too. My father is named Conceit. My daughters have the names of

Remembrance of Wrongs, Hate, Hostility, and Self-justification. The enemies who have imprisoned me are the opposite virtues—Freedom from Anger and Lowliness, while Humility lays a trap for me."

On the eighth step the crown is freedom from anger. He who wears it by nature may never come to wear another. But he who has sweated for it and won it has conquered all eight together.

Step 9

Letting the Past Be Past

In the last chapter we talked about Step Eight **(On Meekness)** and we saw how dangerous anger is for our spiritual ascent towards God. At the end of this discussion I quoted St. John's description of the "daughters" of anger. In Step Nine, he takes up one of these daughters: **Remembrance of wrongs.** He writes:

> **Remembrance of wrongs comes as the final point of anger. It is a keeper of sins. It hates a just way of life. It is the ruin of virtues, the poison of the soul, a worm in the mind. It is the shame of prayer, a cutting off of supplication, a turning away from love, a nail piercing the soul.**

When we become angry, upset, and bothered by the actions of others, if we embrace that anger and claim it as our own (rather than rejecting it as belonging to the devil), if we take it into our hearts and into our souls and nourish it, feeding it with our memory (which has a tendency

to exaggerate what it remembers, tilting it in our favor), we have
practiced what St. John is describing. Remembrance of wrongs is
refusal to forgive; it is planning revenge; it is nourishing hurt
feelings. It is practicing what is called the "broken record" syn-
drome: playing the hurts over and over again in our minds.

St. John is correct in pointing out that this practice is spiritually (and emotionally) destructive. He writes:

**I have seen hatred shatter a . . . relationship, and then
afterwards remembrance of wrongs stood in the way of
restoring the relationship.**

When anger is taken into our hearts and fed by our memory,
it soon pushes every other thing out of our hearts. You cannot
have anger and love in the same heart for long. The nature of
anger is that it is always growing. Have you ever noticed that you
can't stay angry at just one person? Anger against one person
tends to spill over.

Once I have turned the corner and have embarked on my
own self-pity party, I soon begin to notice how many people treat
me poorly and speak to me rudely. I then begin to add them to
my broken record, and my list of offenses grows larger. I become
more angry and more bitter. I become more and more self-
absorbed. I love less and I am able to receive love less. Ultimately,
I become so embittered that I experience no love and I give no
love. *I am alone in hell!* The demons have me just where they want
me to be.

How do I escape from this hell? How do I keep from de-
scending into it in the first place? St. John has lots of good, practical advice. Firstly, he says it is better not to get angry, not to
notice wrongs which have been done against us.

The man who has put a stop to anger has also wiped out remembrance of wrongs.

Secondly, when we get angry (and which of us is at the place where we do not get angry?), we must immediately reject the feelings of anger and disturbance as being Satan-inspired and spiritually destructive.

Forgive quickly and you will be abundantly forgiven. To forget wrongs is to prove oneself truly repentant, but to brood on them and at the same time to imagine one is practicing repentance is to act like the man who is convinced he is running when in fact he is fast asleep.

Thirdly, if we find ourselves unable to forgive the person, we must remind ourselves who is the real source of sin and destruction.

Let your malice and your spite be turned against the devils.

The people who offend us and sin against us are not the real culprits! Satan and his demons are behind every sin and injustice committed in this world. We must pity the one who has been used by Satan, and we must despise Satan. To remember *his* wrongs is spiritually helpful. To remind ourselves constantly of his ability to deceive is to remind ourselves to stay far away from his devices and close to the Holy Church.

Fourthly, if after all of this, we are still unable to rid ourselves of remembrance of wrongs, St. John advises the following:

If after great effort you still fail to root out this thorn, go to your enemy and apologize, if only with empty

words whose insincerity may shame you. Then as conscience, like a fire, comes to give you pain, you may find that a sincere love of your enemy may come to life.

Hard words! But how much harder is hell! In case you don't see how these words apply to you, consider the following:

Never imagine that this dark passion is a passion of no importance, for it often reaches out even to spiritual men.

Such is the ninth step. Let him who has taken it have the courage henceforth to ask Jesus the Savior to free him from his sins.

Step 10

Keeping Our Mouths Shut, Part One

St. John labels the tenth step **On Slander.** His introduction explains the connection with the steps which went before:

> **I imagine that no one with any sense would dispute that slander is the child of hatred and remembrance of wrongs. Hence the need to discuss it next in the order after its forebears.**

What is slander? To slander someone is to speak evil of him behind his back; it is to criticize her and to malign her to others. Very often, as St. John points out, slander is covered over by "pious" intentions:

> **I have rebuked people who were engaged in slander, and, in self-defense, these evildoers claimed to be acting out of love and concern**

for the victim of their slander. My answer to that was to say: "Then stop that kind of love. . . . If, as you insist, you love that man, then do not be making a mockery of him, but pray for him in secret."

For St. John, slander is spiritually dangerous for two reasons. Firstly, because it is hypocritical:

It puts on the appearance of love and is the ambassador of an unholy and unclean heart.

Very often when we slander others we practice the worst kind of deceit. The person whom we are slandering knows nothing of our dislike or disagreement. We say nothing to him. Yet, when he is not around, we speak of him negatively to others. This is duplicity. Putting others down can also be a way that we build ourselves up. It makes us look good (pious, intelligent, etc.) to be able to point out the bad in someone else. It often puts us into the good graces of others when we join them in their slander.

Notice how we thus use others for our own gain when we act this way. Our concern is not for the one we slander (we would speak to her first if it were), nor is our concern for the safety of the ones to whom we speak—our concern is for ourselves! We look good at the expense of someone else. How far have we strayed from the path of divine love and self-sacrifice! The Bible says: *Love will cover a multitude of sins* (1 Pet. 4:8). True love covers the "nakedness," the sin, of our father or brother. But like Ham, don't we often expose it instead? Don't we often delight in pointing out the mistakes of others? And the worst part of it is that we most often do this with regard to pious and holy things.

Contemporary Orthodoxy is riddled with this kind of

slander. How often do we fall into the trap of criticizing what someone else in the Orthodox world is doing or saying? The most pious ones are often the guiltiest! After Liturgy, we gather in our halls and talk about what this bishop has said or not said, what this priest has changed or not changed, what this parish is doing or not doing . . . How truly awful! Under the guise of pious talk, we slander our fathers and brothers. With our tongue,

> . . . *we bless our God and Father, and with it we curse men, who have been made in the similitude of God. Out of the same mouth proceed blessing and cursing. My brethren, these things ought not to be so (James 3:9, 10).*

I remember the example of one holy nun I spent time with. Someone with me asked her a question about what someone else was teaching. It was a serious question, and the questioner's spiritual life was directly in the balance. The nun had inside information about the instructor because she had taken several courses from him.

I watched that holy woman struggle intensely trying to tell the person not to take any courses from that instructor without saying anything negative about him. Somehow she managed to tell the questioner not to take the course without lowering his opinion of the instructor. She made so many excuses for the instructor that you left knowing that although he could not be trusted as an authentic witness to the Orthodox Faith, he still was a man made in the image of God who needed, not our condemnation, but our prayers. The nun also was quick to condemn herself in the process, so that we had no temptation to join her in judgment of another.

This pious example has stuck with me. The nun struggled so

much not to say anything negative about an instructor (someone in a position of authority), and only spoke at all because someone's spiritual life was in danger. She had no concern for herself, but was only concerned for the persons about whom and to whom she was speaking. This is true love. This is holiness and sanctity.

A good grape picker chooses to eat ripe grapes and does not pluck what is unripe. A charitable and sensible mind takes careful note of the virtues it observes in another, while the fool goes looking for faults and defects.

Secondly, St. John condemns slander because of the attitude which lies behind it. Slander is the fruit of a judgmental spirit. The Apostle James identifies the connection:

> *Do not speak evil of one another, brethren. He who speaks evil of a brother and judges his brother, speaks evil of the law and judges the law. But if you judge the law, you are not a doer of the law but a judge. There is one Lawgiver, who is able to save and to destroy. Who are you to judge another? (James 4:11, 12).*

When we judge others we make ourselves equal to God. In so doing, we invite His strict judgment. We enter into competition with Him, and in this position we are bound to lose! When we refuse to judge others, we make ourselves His inferiors. In this position, we invite His mercy and compassion. We make no claims for ourselves, but confess ourselves to be equal to the greatest of sinners. In this position we emerge as victorious.

St. John, to encourage us to refuse to judge others, points out how very often our judgments are incorrect.

Do not condemn. Not even if your very eyes are seeing something, for they may be deceived.

Given the finitude of our minds and knowledge, we see all things, not as they are in fulfillment, but as they are in process. And things in process often look very different than they do in fulfillment. Some of the world's greatest masterpieces looked very ugly halfway through!

Do not start passing judgment on the offender—Judas was one of the company of Christ's disciples and the robber was in the company of killers. Yet what a turnabout there was when the decisive moment arrived!

We do not know the end and we certainly cannot read others' hearts.

I knew a man who sinned openly but repented in secret. I denounced him for being lecherous but he was chaste in the eyes of God, having propitiated Him by a genuine conversion.

Only God knows the heart of man. When we judge others, we often condemn those whom God has already forgiven. We oppose God's mercy with our own justice. And remember:

Judgment is without mercy to the one who has shown no mercy. Mercy triumphs over judgment (James 2:13).

To pass judgment on another is to usurp shamelessly a prerogative of God, and to condemn is to ruin one's soul.

A judgmental spirit also carries with it a spiritual boomerang.

Those who pass speedy and harsh judgments on the sins
of their neighbors fall into this passion.... It is the mur-
dering demons who push us into sin. If they are balked
here, they get us to pass judgment on those who are sin-
ning, thereby smearing us with the stain we are de-
nouncing in others.

There are certain laws which govern the spiritual realm even
as natural laws govern the physical. One of these is that what we
judge others for, we will soon be guilty of ourselves.

So listen to me, all you accountants of other people's
faults, listen well; for ... whatever sin of body or spirit
that we ascribe to our neighbor we will surely fall into
ourselves.

For all of us who struggle with this dangerous sin, St. John has
direct advice:

Do not allow human respect to get in your way when
you hear someone slandering his neighbor. Instead, say
this to him, "Brother, stop it! I do worse things every
day, so how can I criticize him?" You accomplish two
things when you say this. You heal yourself and you heal
your neighbor with the one bandage.

Do not make judgments and you will travel no
quicker road to the forgiveness of your sins.

This is the tenth step, and he who succeeds in it has
practiced love or mourning.

STEP 11

KEEPING OUR MOUTHS SHUT, PART TWO

We now come to Step Eleven: **On Talkativeness And Silence.** It is easy to see how Step Ten **(On Slander)** leads us to Step Eleven. St. John explains it this way:

> The brief discussion in the previous chapter was concerned with the great danger of passing judgment on others, or rather with being judged and being punished by one's own tongue, and it touched on the fact that this vice can lay hold of the most apparently spiritual people.
>
> The time has come now to indicate the cause of this vice and to give an adequate account of the door by which it enters—or, more accurately, by which it goes out.

What is the cause of slander? It is quite simply that we

exercise very little (if any) control over our tongues. In short, we talk too much.

Talkativeness is spiritually dangerous. St. John says:

Talkativeness is the throne of vainglory on which it loves to preen itself and show off. Talkativeness is a sign of ignorance, a doorway to slander, a leader of jesting, a servant of lies, the ruin of compunction, a summoner of despondency, a messenger of sleep, a dissipation of recollection, the end of vigilance, the cooling of zeal, the darkening of prayer.

On the other hand, silence brings with it great spiritual benefit.

Intelligent silence is the mother of prayer, freedom from bondage, custodian of zeal, a guard on our thoughts, a watch on our enemies, a prison of mourning, a friend of tears, a sure recollection of death, a painter of punishment, a concern with judgment, servant of anguish, foe of license, a companion of stillness, the opponent of dogmatism, a growth of knowledge, a hand to shape contemplation, hidden progress, the secret journey upward.

St. John's words remind us of the instruction of the Apostle James:

So then, my beloved brethren, let every man be swift to hear, slow to speak . . . (James 1:19).

To ascend to God we must be silent! Talkativeness will lead us to hell.

How hard it is for us Americans to implement the wisdom of these words! As a society we are very uncomfortable with silence.

Noise is everywhere! What is the first thing most Americans do when they get into their cars? Turn on the radio. What is the first thing most Americans do when they get home? Turn on the television set.

We fear silence, and we surround ourselves with noise. Why? Because we are afraid of what silence brings. Silence makes us pay attention to ourselves. Silence reveals to us the thoughts and intents of our hearts. We are externally directed people, taking our cues from outside. To face what is truly inside, to stop listening to others, to escape the distraction of external noise, to stop talking and to be silent is a fearful proposition.

Yet this is exactly what we must do if we are going to ascend to heaven. We must come to grips with who we are. And we must be quiet if we are going to hear God's directions.

The lover of silence draws close to God. He talks to Him in secret and God enlightens him. Jesus, by His silence, shamed Pilate; and a man, by his stillness, conquers vainglory.

Anyone who has tried to practice this virtue knows that it is very difficult to be silent. St. James reminds us:

No man can tame the tongue. It is an unruly evil, full of deadly poison (James 3:8).

Why is it so difficult to control our mouths? Why is silence so hard for us to practice? First, we often talk too much because we are undisciplined, lazy people. St. John says:

The tongue is a member of the body, like the rest, and therefore needs to be trained in its habits.

Talkativeness is to the mouth what gluttony is to the belly. Overtalking comes from the same source as overeating. We are lazy people who give in to our passions. We are undisciplined and do not exercise control over our bodily members. How often do we think before we speak? How often do we ask ourselves: "Should I be talking now? Is there a reason for talking? Can anything good come from what I have to say?"

I think most of us think of talking as we think of breathing. It is for most of us an involuntary movement of the body. The idea that we need to control our tongues and that it might be better for us to say nothing rather than something is a novel one to our experience. Yet this is necessary for our spiritual growth and health. St. John reminds us:

> **Peter wept bitterly for what he had said. He had forgotten the one who declared: "I said: I will guard my ways so that I may not sin with my tongue" (Ps. 38:1). He had forgotten too the saying, "Better to fall from a height to the ground than to slip with the tongue" (Ecclus. 20:18).**

Secondly, we often talk too much because we are proud. Let's face it, we usually talk because we think that what we have to say is important. We share our opinions because we think they are right. We usually speak so as to inform and to teach others. And we are most often very quick to share our opinions about everything and everyone.

Think about the amount of pride that lies behind our words. Perhaps I am driving through town and I see a house painted a strange color. Why do I feel the need to comment on it? Why do I allow the negative statement to come out of my mouth? Just because I think it is strange, does that mean it *is* strange? Am I a better judge of what a good color for a house is than the people who live in the house? Perhaps I am trying to impress the person with whom I am traveling. Isn't this also pride?

And we do this all the time. We act as if the world is just dying for our opinions about everything. Someone is having a conversation. Why do we enter into it? Usually because we think we have something to add. Isn't this pride? Wouldn't it be better to be quiet? Are we the saviors of the world who have been placed here to deliver our friends and family members from false opinions? We don't often think this way, but perhaps we should. St. John says:

Talkativeness is the throne of vainglory on which it loves to preen itself and show off.

At least for me, his words are too close for comfort.

When I am driving somewhere with my family, I often play a game with my children. We call it the quiet game. In this game we see who can go the longest without talking. (I usually lose!) Perhaps it would do us all good to play this game more often. As Thumper's mother in the movie *Bambi* reasoned: "If you can't say something nice, don't say anything at all."

It is hard to keep water in without a dike. But it is harder still to hold in one's tongue.

This is the eleventh step. He who succeeds in taking it has with one blow cut off a host of evils.

STEP 12

SPEAKING THE TRUTH

St. John introduces Step 12 in this way:

From flint and steel comes fire; from chatter and joking comes lying. Lying is the destruction of charity, and perjury the very denial of God.

Telling the truth! My guess is that we all are familiar with the importance of this virtue. And yet how often do we downplay or excuse our lack of honesty! My observation, both of myself and of our contemporary society, is that we have become desensitized to lying. No longer do our consciences bother us when we are less than honest. We shade the truth so as not to hurt others' feelings, and we feel no remorse. We exaggerate a little here and a little there so as to make ourselves look better to others, and we experience no sorrow. We tell an out-and-out untruth, and we do not remember it as sin when we go to the sacrament of confession. Worse yet, we often justify our lying and excuse it as being "necessary" and perhaps even "justified."

St. John expresses the wisdom of the Fathers:

> **A man may lie on the grounds of prudence and indeed regards as an act of righteousness the actual destruction of his own soul. The inventor of lies declares that he is following the example of Rahab and maintains that his own destruction is the cause of salvation for others.**
>
> **Only when we are completely free of the urge to lie may we resort to it, and then only in fear and out of necessity.**

In another place he writes:

> **No sensible man imagines that lying is a minor failing. Indeed, the All-Holy Spirit pronounced the most dreadful sentence on this sin above all others; and if, as David says to God, "You will destroy everyone speaking a lie" (Ps. 5:7), what will happen to those who swear to their lies on oath?**

Why is desensitization to truth so spiritually dangerous? The key issue here is our hearts. Every time we lie, shading or stretching the truth, our hearts become spiritually confused. Falsehood divides our hearts, making them unstable, spiritually unsteady. If we continue to live a lifestyle of falsehood, we become internally disconnected from the truth. We all know the extreme cases where people are no longer able to know the difference between truth and lies. What we might not know is that every time we tell a lie, we blur our own ability to apprehend the truth.

And remember, when we talk about truth as Orthodox

Christians we are not talking about an abstract concept; we are talking rather about a Person who declared Himself to be *the Way, the Truth and the Life* (John 14:6). God is the author of Truth because He is Truth. Satan is, according to the Scriptures, the father of lies (see John 8:44). The more we tell the truth, the more pure our hearts become, and the more surely and intimately do we know God. Notice I said, "know God," not "know about God"! Anyone can know about God, but only those pure in heart are allowed to see God.

In Psalm 24 (23, LXX) we read:

Who may ascend into the hill of the Lord?
Or who may stand in His holy place?
He who has clean hands and a pure heart,
Who has not lifted up his soul to an idol,
Nor sworn deceitfully.

We should not understand these words to represent some sort of legal requirement which must be met before we can enter into God's presence. They are not abstract legal requirements at all. They are spiritual requirements. Without clean hands and a pure heart, without complete dedication to the true God, without honesty and habitual truth-telling, we *cannot* ascend to or stand in His presence. Not because He doesn't want us there or will somehow keep us out because He is angry with us for our sin, but, on a much deeper and more intense level, because we are unprepared to face the God who is absolute Truth and absolute Purity. As fire burns up chaff, so too the splendor of His absolute divinity will destroy the sinful hypocrisy of our hearts.

As like seeks like, if our hearts are used to falsehood, we will

seek the presence of Satan and avoid the presence of God. But, if
our hearts are accustomed to Truth, we will flee from the presence of Satan and pursue the presence of God.

These considerations lead us to an important point. You can
easily see how foreign to this true way of looking at salvation is
the Protestant theory of "imputed" or "forensic" righteousness.
The problem in our salvation is not the fulfillment of some abstract legal requirements which have been established by God.
The problem in our salvation is our hearts. God desires us to be
with Him; but to be with Him in our sinful, fallen state is
impossible.

This is why God led Adam and Eve out of the Garden: to
protect them from His purity and the absolute splendor of His
divinity. All of the Old Testament ceremonial regulations had
this as their goal: to protect the people of God from premature
contact with the splendor of His divinity. Remember what happened to Uzzah when he touched the ark of the covenant (2 Sam.
6:6, 7)?

This is why it was necessary for God to find a pure human
being before He could become flesh. This is why the Church
delights in and sings of the purity of the Mother of God. Her
purity was an essential component of His Incarnation. We sing
of this over and over again, and we marvel at the fact that her
womb contained the fire of His divinity without being consumed
by it—just as we marvel at the bush which burned without being
consumed and at the three holy children who walked in the fire
without being consumed.

As we travel through this world of sin and death, our goal is
to prepare ourselves for the indwelling of God. This is the *purpose* of all of our spiritual labors: to prepare ourselves to receive

the God of God, who is the Light of Lights and the Truth of Truths!

Think back about everything you hear each Lent. Isn't this what the service books say?

> *Let us sanctify our souls and purify our flesh . . . and let us faithfully persevere in this so that we may be worthy to see the joy of His holy Resurrection (Vespers for Clean Monday).*

The message is clear: to experience the joy, we must prepare ourselves by sanctifying our souls and purifying our flesh.

It is true, as we celebrate each year in its fullness at Pascha, that Jesus paid it all. It is true that Jesus has fully accomplished everything that is necessary for my salvation. But it is equally true that I must make myself ready to receive His grace.

> *He who would love life*
> *And see good days,*
> *Let him refrain His tongue from evil,*
> *And His lips from speaking deceit (1 Pet. 3:10).*

This is the twelfth step. The man who has taken it has obtained the root of all blessings.

STEP 13

ESCAPING FROM BOREDOM

St. John calls the thirteenth step of the Ladder, **Tedium of the spirit.** What is tedium of spirit? He explains it in this way:

> **Tedium is a paralysis of the soul, a slackness of the mind, a neglect of religious exercises, a hostility to vows taken. It is an approval of worldly things.**

The word for despondency in the Greek is *akidia,* and it indicates a listlessness or torpor. The best English word that I can think of to explain it is the word *boredom*, or perhaps we could even use the word *distraction*.

Very often, it begins as a loss of a sense of purpose and ends in despair and spiritual death. St. John's examples should strike home to us.

> **When dinner is ready, he [the Christian] jumps out of his bed. But now when the time for prayer**

comes, his body begins to languish once more again. He begins his prayers, but the tedium makes him sleepy and the verses of the psalms are snatched from his mouth by untimely yawns.

Is there any one of us who has not experienced this more than once?

When the psalms do not have to be sung, tedium does not arise, and the Office is hardly over when the eyes are ready to open again. . . .

Note how tedium hits you when you are standing, and if you sit down, it suggests that it would be a good thing to lean back. It suggests that you prop yourself up against the walls of your cell. It produces noise and foot-steps—and there you go peeping out of the window.

Once again, is there anyone among us who has not lived this? In our day and age, this demon is very much at work. How often does he confuse us with the suggestion that our spiritual labors are in vain? How often does he suggest to us that our efforts are accomplishing no good result? How often does he point out to us many others who seem to be gaining ground without laboring as hard as we are? How often does he suggest that we shouldn't take the spiritual life quite so seriously? How often does he remind us of our failures and suggest that perhaps we are wasting our time in pursuing the spiritual life? How often does he weigh our hearts down with earthly cares and thoughts even in the midst of our prayers? How often does he encourage us to take a day off, to sleep in and skip our prayers, to take a spiritual vacation? After all, he says, what harm can a few days of relaxation and fun do? How often does the demon of boredom confuse our thoughts so that we forget what the goal is and how we are to achieve it? We know the answer: too many times.

How do we battle this demon? St. John suggests two things: **perseverance in the course taken** and **cooperation with others who are struggling.** The only way to beat boredom is to labor through it. St. John writes:

> **The real men of spirit can be seen at the time when tedium strikes, for nothing gains so many crowns for a monk as the struggle against this.**

We modern Christians tend to be "flash-in-the-pan" people. We start things, do them for a while, and then start something new. This is not the approved method for living the spiritual life. What is needed is *perseverance* and finishing the course. Once we have started on a certain path of prayer and struggle, we must keep on keeping on without allowing ourselves to be distracted.

Secondly, we beat boredom by reminding ourselves of what others have done and are doing. **Tedium,** says St. John, **is rebuffed by community life.** In our day and age, it is important that we continuously remind ourselves of the labors of the saints. Nothing beats tedium as much as the stories of the saints. All of the demon's suggestions are answered by the examples of these holy ones. In addition, it is good for us to establish relationships with others who are struggling. Knowing that I am not alone, that I am part of a community of strugglers, gives me the encouragement and motivation to persevere when I feel like quitting.

Listen to the words of Tedium as she explains herself:

I cannot lay my head among those who are truly

obedient, and I live quietly where I may. I have many mothers—Stolidity of Soul, Forgetfulness of the Things of Heaven, or sometimes, Too Heavy a Burden of Troubles. My children who live with me are Changing from Place to Place, Disobedience to One's Superior, Forgetfulness of the Judgment to Come, and sometimes, the Abandonment of One's Vocation. The singing of psalms and manual labor are my opponents by whom I am now bound. My enemy is the thought of death, but what really slays me is prayer backed by a firm hope in the blessings of the future.

This is the thirteenth victory. He who has won it is really outstanding in all virtue.

STEP 14

CONTROLLING OUR EATING HABITS

Step 14, according to St. John, is **Gluttony**. His introduction of the topic is very telling:

> **Gluttony is hypocrisy of the stomach. Filled, it moans about scarcity; stuffed and crammed, it wails about its hunger. Gluttony thinks up seasonings, creates sweet recipes. Stop one urge and another bursts out; stop that one and you unleash yet another. Gluttony has a deceptive appearance: it eats moderately but wants to gobble everything at the same time.**

We are all, I am sure, familiar enough with the urges of gluttony. But perhaps we have not stopped to consider fully the spiritual dangers of gluttony. This is something St. John spends a great deal of time discussing. His analysis is very helpful, for he opens up to us the interconnectedness of the various aspects of the spiritual life. St. John expresses the teaching of the Fathers in this way:

14

The belly is the cause of all human shipwreck.

Why? For two reasons: first, a gluttonous lifestyle feeds the passions which are inherent in man. Unrestrained eating habits spill over into an unrestrained lifestyle. The reason for this is clear:

Gluttony is the prince of the passions.

St. John gives several examples:

- If you struggle with unclean thoughts, remember:
  The mind of someone intemperate is filled with unclean longings.

- If you struggle with talking too much, remember:
  The tongue flourishes where food is abundant.

- If you struggle with a lack of repentance, remember:
  A full stomach dries up one's weeping.

- If you struggle with sexual sin, remember:
  The man who looks after his belly and at the same time hopes to control the passion of fornication is like someone trying to put out a fire with oil.

Of course, these are just a few examples of many. The point which St. John is making may be summarized as follows: The passions with which you struggle are energized by your gluttonous habits. Gluttony feeds your passions. Fasting takes away their nourishment.

Please notice: The nature of the spiritual life is that all passions are interconnected. We cannot allow even one passion to be unrestrained. This is especially true of gluttony. If we are gluttonous, we will be overwhelmed by other passions as well. And what is true in a negative way is also true in a positive way. If we struggle with gluttony and gain some victory, we also gain victory over our other passions.

But gluttony is not dangerous only because it unleashes our passions; the Fathers also teach that gluttony is dangerous because the demon of gluttony is a front man for other, more dangerous demons. Counsels St. John:

> **You should remember that frequently a demon can take up residence in your belly and keep a man from being satisfied, even after having devoured the whole of Egypt and after having drunk the whole of the Nile. After we have eaten, this demon goes off and sends the spirit of fornication against us, saying, "Get him now! Go after him. When his stomach is full, he will not put up much of a fight." Laughing, the spirit of fornication, that ally of the stomach's demon, comes, binds us hand and foot in sleep, does anything he wants with us, befouls body and soul with his dirty dreams and emissions.**

How seldom do we consider this when we are moved to eat! We have been taught to believe everything our body tells us about its needs and desires. Our modern "evolutionary" world has taught us that the body is pure and can experience no evil desires. We assume this to be the case, not knowing that very often the body's desires are demonic desires.

St. John reveals a great deal about the nature of gluttony when he allows her to speak:

> **Why are you complaining, you who are my servants? How is it that you are trying to get away from me? The reason for my being insatiable is habit. Unbroken habit,**

dullness of soul, and the failure to remember death are
the roots of my passion. And how is it that you are looking for the names of my offspring? For if I were to count
them, their number would be greater than the total of
the grains of sand. Still, you may learn at least the names
of my firstborn and beloved children. My firstborn son
is the servant of Fornication, the second is Hardness
of Heart, and the third is Sleepiness. From me flow a
sea of Dirty Thoughts, waves of Filth, floods of unknown and unspeakable Impurities. My daughters are
Laziness, Talkativeness, Breezy Familiarity, Jesting,
Facetiousness, Contradiction, Stubbornness, Contempt, Disobedience, Stolidity of Mind, Captivity,
Boastfulness, Audacity, Love of Worldly Things, followed by Impure Prayer, Distracted Thoughts, and sudden and often unexpected Catastrophes, with which is
linked that most evil of all my daughters, namely, Despair.

Victory over this vice is a brave one. He who is able to
achieve it should hasten towards dispassion and total
chastity.

STEP 15

KEEPING OURSELVES PURE

Step 15 of the Ladder is entitled **Chastity.** St. John of the Ladder writes about the struggle for this virtue in this way:

> **The man who decides to struggle against his flesh and to overcome it by his own efforts is fighting in vain. The truth is that unless the Lord overturns the house of the flesh and builds the house of the soul, the man wishing to overcome it has watched and fasted for nothing. Offer the Lord the weakness of your nature. Admit your incapacity and, without your knowing it, you will win for yourself the gift of chastity.**

St. John promises, **you will win for yourself the gift of chastity.** Sadly, in today's world, these words sound foreign. As a society, we have abandoned the concept of sexual virtue. On our television screens and in the movie

theaters, we calmly watch without reaction repeated violations of
chastity. We hear of our national leaders' sexual adventures and
we experience no repulsion. We engage in sexual sin with almost
no remorse.

As Christians living in this sexually oriented and active world,
it is easy to become desensitized. It is easy to forget that chastity
is a necessary virtue for us to obtain in our ascent to heaven. Holy
Scripture makes this clear:

> *Now the works of the flesh are evident, which are: adultery,
> fornication, uncleanness, lewdness . . . and the like; of which I
> tell you beforehand, just as I also told you in time past, that
> those who practice such things will not inherit the kingdom of
> God (Gal. 5:19, 21).*

St. John of the Ladder calls sexual sin **a sort of death within
us, a sin that is catastrophic.**

What is chastity? St. John answers:

**The chaste man is not someone with a body undefiled,
but rather a person whose members are in complete sub-
jection to the soul.**

The struggle for chastity begins with controlling the body's
sexual desires. It ends with the transfiguration of the body's sexual
desires. This is what St. John means when he says:

**A chaste man is someone who has driven out bodily love
by means of divine love, who has used heavenly fire to
quench the fires of the flesh.**

This struggle for transfiguration takes different paths. For
the unmarried, it is a direct assault on the passions of the flesh.

The mission is to seek and destroy all passionate desire, and through the death of sexual desire to find its transfiguration in the joy of heavenly love. It is full-scale warfare against the flesh, which in the words of St. John, is both **enemy and friend.** For the married, the struggle is to attain confinement, and through confinement to achieve transfiguration.

The goal of both the married and the unmarried is the same: not the repression of natural desire, but its transfiguration through fulfillment. Both the married and the unmarried will end up living sexually transfigured lives in the Kingdom: for in the Kingdom, there is neither marriage nor giving in marriage, but all are like the angels. Of course, only the saints are able to achieve that goal in this world. They live in the Kingdom while still on the earth. The rest of us sinners embrace the struggle to remain chaste and pure in an unchaste and impure world.

In Christian marriage, sexual relationships become part of the transfiguration process. We deal with our bodily passions first by containing them within the confines of marriage. If our sexual passion is thought of as a wild animal, then marriage is the cage by which the wild animal is restrained. In marriage, once the animal has been restrained, it is then transfigured by the reality of divine love. The bodily aspects and physical enjoyments of the sexual relationship become less and less important. "Sex" is no longer the goal; it is the relationship of love which becomes the focus. The union of persons becomes the goal and the sexual relationship finds its meaning in establishing a place for the union to be physically actualized (see 1 Cor. 6:16). The immature trappings of physical love (i.e., sexy nightgowns, romantic lights, etc.) fade away as unnecessary and counterfeit. What predominates is the expression of love, of giving and receiving, of finding joy in bringing joy to another, of experiencing absolute freedom in the context of absolute commitment. Mature sexual love in marriage reaches the place of dispassion without necessarily ceasing to be physical.

Because we are Americans, it is important for me immediately to add a disclaimer. *None of this happens by imposition.* We don't all of a sudden decide to become dispassionate, nor do we disdain the less mature expressions of physical and sexual love in marriage. We certainly don't become obsessed with guilt in marital love. This is a growth process. And, because there are two involved, it is very complicated. Truly, in marriage, it is without knowing it that we win the gift of chastity.

How? This is the key. Firstly, by embracing the concept that physical pleasure is not the primary purpose of the sexual relationship and that sex itself is a means to an end, rather than the end. Secondly, by concentrating on the relationship of love rather than the sexual relationship. This means that in marriage it is necessary for us to exercise self-control and self-restraint. It is necessary even in marriage to curb our desires, to restrain them, to **submit the desires of the body to the demands of the soul.**

For those who are not married, this restraint must of necessity be more severe and more intense. As I said before, it is all-out warfare. The fact is: either you control your sexual desires or they will destroy you. Marriage is a cage in which the grace of God contains the releasing of sexual passion. Outside of marriage, the unleashing of sexual desire is completely destructive. It is a fire which is never satisfied. And it takes over a person's thoughts, actions, and intents. It even takes over his dreams, completely defiling him from within.

And the less loving—the less personal—the context of sexual involvement is, the more dangerous and all-consuming the sexual passion becomes. This is why seemingly harmless activities such as masturbation and use of pornography are in reality incredibly disastrous for the spiritual life. Any sexual expression which is exclusively intrapersonal (i.e., by self aimed at the gratification of self) is extremely addictive and unfulfilling. Sexual passion thus released leads either to greater sexual sin (i.e., fornication and/or homosexuality) and/or to ever greater addiction to the masturbation and pornography.

Of course, the same is true of casual sex. Casual sex is really another expression of intrapersonal sex; the partner is not important as a person, but only as a body which allows one to experience the physical pleasure of the sexual relationship. Since there is no relationship of love, sexual passion, once released, becomes obsessive. Ultimately life becomes exclusively sexual; everyone (including both sexes and children) and everything (including the animal kingdom) becomes an acceptable body for one to experiment with and find physical pleasure through. In this life of exclusive sexuality, the higher concepts of love and friendship and compassion and spirituality are lost. Man becomes an animal.

In less blatant and pronounced form, the same thing is true of all sexual relationships outside of blessed, sacramental Christian marriage. Lacking the restraining grace of God and the full nature of marital commitment, the unleashing of sexual passion ultimately consumes the person who allows its release.

How do we fight against this? St. John of the Ladder speaks a great deal of the necessity of doing serious battle against the evil thoughts which we allow into our minds.

Never brood by day over the fantasies that have occurred to you during sleep.

Chastity begins in the mind! St. John also insists that we must never allow ourselves to hear or look at anything unchaste.

We should strive in all possible ways neither to see nor to hear of that fruit we have vowed never to taste. It amazes me to think we could imagine ourselves to be stronger than the prophet David, something quite impossible indeed.

This cannot be stressed enough in today's world. Set a rule for yourself that you will never change: that you will never allow yourself to watch or listen to anything unchaste. Tertullian's rule is a good one to follow: never watch anything you could not do. Yet how often do we do this! In our television and movie watching, do we allow ourselves to watch unchaste actions between unmarried men and women? How often have I heard: "Well, there was only one sex scene in it." *That is one sex scene too many!* Or, "There is only partial nudity in it." *Partial nudity is too much!* We have to be very severe with ourselves if we want to be chaste. Do we think that we are spiritually stronger than David, who fell into adultery and murder just by looking at a naked woman? How about our music? How much of it talks about and describes unchaste behavior? Any is too much! To paraphrase our Lord: It is better to hear no music than to go to hell with headphones on! When we are tempted by our flesh,

... our best weapons are sackcloth and ashes, all-night vigils standing up, hunger, the merest touch of water when we are thirsty, time passed among the burial places

of the dead, and most important of all, humility of heart; and if possible a spiritual director or helpful brother, old in wisdom rather than years, should also support us.

How can we defeat the passions of our body and attain their transfiguration? St. John has the flesh give us the answer:

Within me is my begetter, the love of self. The fire that comes to me from outside is too much pampering and care. The fire within me is past ease and things long done. I conceived and gave birth to sins, and they when born beget death by despair in their turn. And yet if you have learned the sure and rooted weakness within both you and me, you have manacled my hands. If you starve your longings, you have bound my feet, and they can travel no further. If you have taken up the yoke of obedience, you have cast my yoke aside. If you have taken possession of humility, you have cut off my head.

This is the fifteenth reward of victory. He who has earned it while still alive has died and been resurrected. From now on he has a taste of the immortality to come.

STEPS 16 & 17

LETTING GO OF THE THINGS THAT HOLD US

17
16

In this chapter, we will be looking at Steps 16 and 17 of the spiritual Ladder. I am choosing to look at these together because they represent opposite sides of the same coin. Step 16 describes the spiritual illness, while Step 17 prescribes the spiritual cure. The words of Jesus fittingly introduce their theme:

> Do not lay up for yourselves treasures on earth ... but lay up for yourselves treasures in heaven ... For where your treasure is, there your heart will be also (Matt. 6:19–21).

There is very little which reveals the state of our hearts more clearly than the way we use our financial possessions. Talk is cheap! It is easy to say that we are living for heaven. Our bank accounts and check registers demonstrate the veracity of our claim. Are we living for the Kingdom, or do the things of this world predominate and consume us?

St. John warns us of the spiritual danger of money and possessions in Step 16, which he labels **Avarice**. His words of description are brief, but full of insight:

> **Avarice is a worship of idols and is the offspring of unbelief. It makes excuses for infirmity and is the mouthpiece of old age.**

In these words St. John strikes at the heart of the matter. Do we trust in God, or do we trust in our financial portfolio? Do we believe that God can and will take care of our needs as we do really seek first His Kingdom? Does the future belong to Him or to our financial planner? There is a spiritual reality here:

> **The man who has conquered this vice [of avarice] has cut out care, but the man trapped by it can never pray freely to God.**

The more we have, the more complicated our lives become. The more things we own, the more we have to worry about their care and preservation. All of these issues, although not sinful or wrong, are distracting and keep us from pursuing the one thing which alone is needful. The simpler we can make our lives, the more we can lower our financial obligations, the freer we become, the fewer cares we have, and the more we can pursue God undistractedly! St. John says, in words which we all understand:

> **Waves never leave the sea. Anger and gloom never leave the miserly.**

Of course, all of this comes by way of spiritual counsel and guidance rather than legalistic laws or rules. Financial possessions are not sinful in and of themselves. Having lots of things is not incompatible with the higher spiritual life. It just makes it more difficult. St. John explains:

The man who has tasted the things of heaven easily thinks nothing of what is below, but he who has had no taste of heaven finds pleasure in possessions.

The man of charity spreads his money about him, but the man who claims to possess both charity and money is a self-deceived fool. . . . A generous man met a miser, and the miser said the other man was without discernment.

In addition to making our lives more difficult and spiritually distracting, material possessions also can make us insensitive to the needs of others around us. How often have I observed this to be the case! With each step up the financial ladder, with each new purchase, with each new assumption of debt, people have less and less money to share. This is the "American dream," which in our modern day and age has become the "American debtors' prison."

As salaries increase, instead of living simply and giving more away, we Americans spend more and increase our debt load. The more we make, the less we have to give away. St. John notes this:

The collector [of money] is stirred by charity, but, when the money is in, the grip tightens.

This grip ultimately becomes so tight that it strangles our hearts, taking away the breath of the soul, which is love for God and for the image of God in one's neighbor. St. John summarizes:

> **Avarice . . . causes hatred, theft, envy, separations, hostility, stormy blasts, remembrance of past wrongs, inhuman acts and even murder.**

It is a serious sickness!

What then is its cure? Step 17 prescribes it: **Poverty**. Listen to the words of St. John:

> **Poverty . . . is resignation from care. It is life without anxiety and travels light, far from sorrow and faithful to the commandments. The poor monk is lord of the world. He has handed all his cares over to God, and by his faith has obtained all men as his servants. If he lacks something he does not complain to his fellows and he accepts what comes his way as if from the hand of the Lord. In his poverty he turns into a son of detachment and he sets no value on what he has.**

For the monk, this poverty is absolute. The true monk owns nothing, having forsaken it all in his pursuit of God. For those of us who live in the world, this poverty is approximate. We have obligations (mouths to feed, bodies to clothe, shelter to obtain) and we must fulfill these obligations. It seems to me that poverty is best approximated in our position by striving to reduce the number of our obligations.

What we should be aiming at is the simple life. Notice I did not say a life of deprivation. For us beginners in the spiritual life, severe deprivation can be as distracting as financial prosperity. I find the words of Agur to reveal the royal way:

> *Give me neither poverty nor riches—*
> *Feed me with the food allotted to me;*
> *Lest I be full and deny You,*
> *And say, "Who is the Lord?"*
> *Or lest I be poor and steal,*
> *And profane the name of my God (Prov. 30:8, 9).*

In practical terms, this certainly must mean that I strive hard to reduce my debt load, live on what I make, and resist the temptation to allow my spending to increase in proportion to my income. As my income grows, I should give more away rather than spending more on myself. Thus, ultimately, we see the great importance of charitable giving. For us in the world, it is a very true statement that our salvation depends on our almsgiving. We cannot live in absolute poverty (though some of us seem to be awfully close sometimes). But we can live generously.

Such then is the sixteenth contest, and the man who has triumphed in it has either won love or cut out care.

This is the seventeenth step. He who has climbed it is traveling to heaven unburdened by material things.

STEP 18

GETTING SERIOUS

Step 18 is labeled by St. John as **Insensitivity**. He describes it in the following poetic words:

> **Insensitivity is deadened feeling in body and spirit. . . . Lack of awareness is negligence that has become habit.**

According to St. John, as we pursue the heavenly goal, we need to be aware of the great danger of becoming desensitized to the importance of spiritual realities. St. John describes a scenario familiar to all:

> **The insensitive man . . . complains about what has happened and does not stop eating what is harmful. He prays against it but carries on as before, doing it and being angry with himself. . . . His lips pray against it and his body struggles for it. He talks profoundly about death and acts as if he will never die. . . . He has plenty to say**

about self-control and fights for a gourmet life. He reads
about the judgment and begins to smile, about vainglory
and is vainglorious while he is reading. He recites what
he has learnt about keeping vigil, and at once drops off
to sleep. Prayer he extols, and runs from it as if from a
plague. Blessings he showers on obedience, and he is
the first to disobey. Detachment he praises, and he
shamelessly fights over a rag. . . . He gorges himself, is
sorry, and a little later is at it again. . . . He teaches meekness and frequently gets angry while he is teaching
it. He denounces laughter, and while lecturing on
mourning he is all smiles. In front of others he criti-
cizes himself for being vainglorious, and in making the
admission he is looking for glory. He looks people in
the eye with passion and talks about chastity. . . . He
glorifies almsgivers and despises the poor.

When we are first awakened to the spiritual life and introduced to its depths, we are awestruck and experience a godly fear.
I will never forget the fear and awe which resonated throughout
my entire body when I was given the Lamb of God (the center of
the *prosphora* loaf) to hold in my priestly ordination. I could not
even look upon Christ lying in my hands, and I was moved to
tears by the holiness of the office to which I was being ordained.
I realized that this was no churchly game and no empty ritual. It
was real, and I was holding Christ, the Lamb of God who takes
away the sins of the world. I was standing in heaven. The saints
and the Theotokos were around me. The angel of the altar was
breathing down my neck. How careful I was in my movements,
with what fear did I walk around the altar!

As I have matured in my priesthood, how hard it has been to keep that same sense of awe and godly fear. In this way, perhaps it is true that familiarity breeds contempt. It is a struggle not to become insensitive to the spiritual realities with which I am now familiar. I have to push myself not to allow **lack of awareness** to become a **habit of negligence.**

If this is true for me in my priesthood, I am sure that it is also true for you in your own experience of Orthodoxy. St. John points out through his descriptions several root causes of insensitivity. Insensitivity develops when we allow a division to exist between our words and our actions. This can happen to us very easily.

A few Advents ago, I was invited to attend an early morning discussion group which was meeting to explore the Orthodox understanding of deification. It was a high-powered group of thinkers who carefully talked through the stages of the spiritual journey (purification, illumination, deification) and their meaning for us in our own ascent towards God.

After the discussion time, breakfast was mentioned. Sure enough, soon the griddle was going, the bacon was frying, the eggs were cooking, the donuts were being delivered, and we were preparing for a real feast. *This is what St. John is talking about when he describes insensitivity.* Here we were, after a lengthy discussion on the exalted doctrine of deification, eating bacon, eggs, and doughnuts during a fasting period. Somehow the connection between our words and our actions was lost. We talked about deification and thought that we understood it well, but our actions betrayed our lack of real knowledge.

It is easy to allow our Orthodoxy to become something we talk about. Orthodoxy must be something we *live*. And it is only as we live it sincerely, struggling to practice what we preach and to connect the exalted words we speak to an exalted way of life, that we will be delivered from insensitivity.

What St. John is talking about is that we must never be satisfied with our own experience of Orthodoxy. We must constantly push ourselves. We will always talk better than we live. *But let us always be bothered by this.* Let us repent of this. Let the inconsistencies of our lives be the proverbial burr under the saddle that motivates us out of the comfort of our complacency into living lives of radical obedience to Christ.

I am reminded of a story told by Serge Bokshakoff of his journeys to Finnish monasteries. At one monastery there were several very pious older monks living in community together. Serge had heard reports of their sanctity and spiritual perfection; thus, he was looking forward to asking them questions about the spiritual life. In particular, he wanted to talk to them about the prayer of the heart and the intricacies of hesychasm.

When he got to the monastery, he was allowed to speak to a wise, older hieromonk. Serge posed a question to this man about the prayer of the heart, expecting to get a very reasoned and spiritually beneficial answer. Instead, he received the following:

> I am sorry, but we are poor, sinful men here. It is enough
> for us to pray hard, to forgive often, and to struggle with
> the external aspects of the monastic life. We can't answer
> your question. You'll have to find other, more holy monks
> to give you direction.

The hieromonk is an example to us. Here he was, an experienced struggler, refusing to speak of deep spiritual issues because of his inexperience, and here we are, inexperienced spiritual neophytes, talking about all kinds of spiritual things we haven't experienced at all. It is far better for us to speak of things we know—the struggle to forgive, the struggle to fast, the struggle to love, the struggle to give, the struggle not to judge, the struggle to live a moral life in an immoral world—than to speak of things more exalted which we don't know.

When St. John speaks to Insensitivity, her response is telling:

Those who are under my sway laugh when they see the bodies of the dead. At prayer they are stony, hard, and blinded. In front of the altar they feel nothing. They receive the Holy Gift as if it were ordinary bread. . . . I am the mother of Laughter, the nurse of Sleep, the friend of the Full Stomach. When I am found out I do not grieve, and I am the ally of Fake Piety. . . . Big meals keep me going, time adds to my stature and bad habit fixes me in such a way that he who possesses me will never be rid of me. But if you are always on the watch and think of eternal judgment, maybe I shall let go of you to some extent. If you discover why I came to be within you, it will be possible for you to do battle with my mother, since she is not the same for all. Pray often where the dead are laid out and paint in your heart an indelible image of them, traced there with the brush of fasting. For otherwise you will never defeat me.

Fr. Alexander Schmemann is quoted as saying that the worst sin is to make Orthodoxy into a religion. To reduce it to a set of external rules and rituals which must be performed by rote is the height of insensitivity. Orthodoxy is not a "religion," *it is life!* Let us be serious about this life which we have received. Everything in this Church has meaning. This is no game, this is not make-believe. This is real! Let us not play games with it. Let us not be content to have a life which is only *influenced* by our faith. Let us live lives *controlled* by our faith. Let us get serious.

I have described, as much as my poor talents permit, the wiles and the havoc wrought by this stony, stubborn, raging, ignorant passion, and I refuse to dwell on it. If there is anyone with the God-given skill to heal the sores, let him not shrink from the task.

STEP 19

STAYING AWAKE

There is a saying in the Book of Proverbs which introduces the theme of Step 19 very well:

A little sleep, a little slumber,
A little folding of the hands to sleep—
So shall your poverty come on you like a prowler,
And your need like an armed man.

(Interestingly, this saying occurs twice: Proverbs 6:10, 11
and Proverbs 24:33, 34.)

In Step 19, St. John reminds us that too much sleep,
like too much of anything, can be spiritually dangerous.

**Just as too much drinking comes from habit, so
too from habit comes overindulgence in sleep.
For this reason one has to struggle against it especially at the start of one's religious life, because
a long-standing habit is very difficult to correct.**

Of course, we all need to sleep. Just as we need to eat, so we need to sleep in order to live. Jesus slept! As St. John notes:

Sleep is a natural state. It is also an image of death and a respite of the senses.

But, although sleep is natural and needful,

... like desire it has many sources. That is to say, it comes from nature, from food, from demons, or perhaps in some degree even from prolonged fasting by which the weakened flesh is moved to long for repose.

How we can tell the difference? St. John does not spend a great deal of time in explaining the answer. But he does point us to one important consideration:

Let us observe and we shall find the spiritual trumpet that summons the brethren together visibly is also the signal for the invisible assembly of our foes.

St. John is very practical and down to earth. He simply reminds us: it is too much sleep when it keeps us from fulfilling our rule of prayer. When we choose to sleep rather than to pray—we have entered into the spiritual danger zone. His description of the struggle with sleep sounds very familiar:

Some [demons] stand by our bed and encourage us to lie down again after we have got up.... Others get those at prayer to fall asleep. Still others cause bad and unusual stomachache, while others encourage prattle in the church. Some inspire bad thoughts, others get us to lean against the wall as though we were weary or to start

**yawning over and over again, while still others cause us
to laugh during prayer so as to provoke the anger of God
against us. . . . Others, by sitting on our mouths, shut
them so that we can scarcely open them.**

Many of the Fathers have pointed out that Satan can oppress
us and make us feel more tired than we are in order to keep us
from praying. Have you ever noticed how this happens at night
when it is time to say your rule of prayer before going to bed? All
of a sudden, you are hit with a tremendous sense of fatigue so
that you can barely make it to your bed without falling asleep.
Sometimes, undoubtedly, this is due to natural causes, but more
often than not, it comes from the evil one. It is a trick to get us to
go to bed without prayer.

St. John of Kronstadt points out that if we go to bed without
prayer, we leave our minds and imaginations open for demonic
assault all night! When we are sleeping, we cannot be vigilant
over our thoughts. Our prayer before sleep shuts down the
openings into our minds and hearts. (This is why we pray to our
Guardian Angel and commend ourselves into the hands of Christ
before sleep.)

There is a saying in the life of Fr. Epiphanios of Athens
(+1988) which struck me. The hagiographer notes that Fr.
Epiphanios never went to bed without saying Compline. No
matter how long his day, or how exhausted he was, he never lay
down to sleep without first saying his prayers. This is cited as one
of the key elements in the development of his sanctity, which was
great. In the lives of other saints, the same thing is said of their
morning prayers.

For those of us who are in the initial stages of the spiritual journey, in our struggle with sleep it is necessary that we never choose sleep over prayer. St. John comments:

A furnace tests gold. Prayer tests the zeal of a monk and his love for God.

What should we do when we are absolutely exhausted? From his own struggles, St. Nicolai of Ochrid offers the following advice: Begin to pray. Pray for five minutes. If, at the end of five minutes, the exhaustion remains, shorten your prayers, finish them, and go to sleep. This exhaustion is natural and not of the evil one. If, however, at the end of five minutes, the exhaustion has lifted, finish your prayers. The exhaustion was of the evil one and you have won the victory!

To draw close to God, to drive out the demons—there is a task to be praised!

STEP 20

STAYING ALERT

In our last chapter, I noted St. John's comment:

A furnace tests gold. Prayer tests the zeal of a monk and his love for God.

To pray is not easy; it is a real struggle. I am reminded of a spiritual father's comments to his spiritual daughter, who was complaining about the distraction of her children during prayer. He simply said to her: "If it is not the children, it is the demons. It is never easy to pray undistractedly."

As we labor to ascend to God (understanding that prayer is both the way and the end of the ascent), we must prepare ourselves for the test of prayer. The first battle is getting to the place and time of prayer. This is what St. John talked about in Step 19: overcoming sleep, getting out of bed (or staying out of bed), and actually forcing ourselves to attend to the time of prayer. In Step 20, he talks about the next part of our struggle in prayer, labeling it **On Alertness.**

Alertness begins when we approach the time of prayer.

The bell rings for prayer. The monk who loves God says, "Bravo, bravo." The lazy monk says, "Alas. Alas."

Mealtime reveals the gluttonous, prayer time the lovers of God. The former dance and the latter frown when the table is made ready.

We should not be surprised if we don't feel like praying. This is part of our fallenness, our own sinful condition, the disorientation of our internal selves. There are many times when the desire for prayer is almost nonexistent (at least to our conscious selves). We must rouse ourselves to prayer.

Alertness is doing battle with our laziness and our lack of interest in prayer. Alertness is motivating ourselves to attend to the things of God rather than the things of this world. There is great wisdom in the fact that the Church teaches us to begin our prayer with the following verses from the psalms:

Come, let us worship and fall down before God our King . . .

Alertness is self-talk; it is self-motivation. It is the triumph of the spirit over the body, of the will for God over the will for self. Alertness continues as we pray.

The inexperienced monk is wide awake when talking to his friends but half asleep at prayer time.

At day's end the merchant counts his profits, and the monk does the same when psalmody is over.

The labor of prayer is a labor with the thoughts. Our minds are far too lazy and undisciplined. Instead of directing our thoughts and controlling them, we allow them to run free, here and there, wherever they wish to go. So, during prayer, we find ourselves often thinking about all kinds of other things. How many times have we come to the end of a prayer only to realize that we have no idea what we just said? How many times in the middle of liturgy do we catch ourselves reviewing yesterday's events and planning for the rest of the day?

Alertness is the struggle to control our minds and center them on the one thing that is needful. It is the attempt to center our mind in our heart, to eliminate not only the bad thoughts, but even the good thoughts which distract us from the pursuit of God. *This is not easy!* St. Silouan of the Holy Mountain says:

> Preserving the mind and heart from all extraneous thoughts means prolonged struggle of an extraordinarily difficult and subtle kind (Archimandrite Sophrony, *Saint Silouan the Athonite,* Stavropegic Monastery of St. John the Baptist, Essex, England, 1991, p. 136).

In our beginning attempts we will fail many more times than we succeed, but we must keep up the struggle. For, as St. John promises:

Such then is the twentieth step. He who has climbed it has received light in his heart.

STEP 21

FACING OUR FEARS

Step 21 is labeled, **On Unmanly Fears.** St. John describes this spiritual danger in these words:

> **[Fear] is a lapse from faith that comes from anticipating the unexpected. Fear is danger tasted in advance, a quiver as the heart takes fright before unnamed calamity. Fear is a loss of assurance.**

The kind of spiritual fear which St. John is describing is one which is illustrated fittingly in the lives of the Apostles at the time of the Crucifixion. Their fear of the unknown, their fear of death, their fear of the power of the evil forces, their fear of public opinion kept them from following after Christ. They abandoned Christ in His Passion because they were afraid.

How often does this spiritual phenomenon take place in our lives as well? How often do we not follow the road which Christ has outlined for us to follow because we are afraid? As St. John notes, for each person the fear is slightly different.

Sometimes we fail to follow Christ because we are afraid of what it will cost us. There is a cost associated with each step of the spiritual journey: a further detachment from the things of this world, a new step of faith and trust, a greater reliance upon Christ. When we face those moments of truth in which the cost is made abundantly clear, we can feel very threatened and vulnerable. For so long we have lived in a certain way, for so long our security has been wrapped up in the things and ways that we are now being asked to put aside. The fears can grow very large.

Other times we falter in our journey towards God because we are afraid of the reactions of others. As we grow towards God, we change. Very often these changes are not immediately accepted by those who have known us. (Perhaps they are threatened by our changes; perhaps they are challenged and convicted by them. The reasons vary.) When we move towards God in positive and challenging ways, we run the risk of encountering misunderstanding, abuse, and rejection. Once again, the fears loom large.

Other times we are afraid of our own inability to do that which God has asked us to do. Perhaps we have failed so many times in the past that we are afraid of failing again. It seems easier to do nothing than to step out in obedience to the call of God.

These and many others represent the nature of our fears. But why are we afraid? St. John pushes us to see the "why" behind the "what." He isolates two factors. First, we often are overwhelmed with fear because of our pride.

A proud soul is the slave of cowardice. Trusting only itself, it is frightened by a soul or shadow. . . . The Lord

rightly withdraws His protection from the proud so that the rest of us may not become vain.

I am sure that most of us have experienced what St. John is describing. We are following after Christ, and for a while, by His grace, we are achieving victory. We are accepting the new challenges and continuing to work on the old. As we begin, we are relying upon Him; our prayer life is active, our need for the sacraments strong, our love for God high.

But as we continue, the intensity of our spiritual life begins to wane. As we fall into a new routine, living out the challenges in a less stressful (and less exciting) environment, our faith in God is gradually replaced by faith in self. Very often we don't even notice it. Then God allows a new challenge to come into our lives. Suddenly we are overwhelmed by fear! Why? It is our pride and self-reliance. Trusting only in ourselves, we suddenly realize how small and weak we are. Fear reigns!

How do we overcome this? By exercising true faith. St. John pushes us with these words:

Do not hesitate to go in the dark of night to those places where you are normally frightened. The slightest concession to this weakness means that this childish and absurd malady will grow old with you. So as you go where fright will lay hold of you, put on the armor of prayer, and when you reach the spot, stretch out your hands and flog your enemies with the name of Jesus, since there is no stronger weapon in heaven or on earth. And when you drive the fear away, give praise to the God Who has delivered you, and He will protect you for all eternity, provided you remain grateful.

Secondly, we often are overwhelmed by fear through demonic oppression. St. John describes it in this way:

"My hair and my flesh shuddered" (Job 4:15). These were the words of Eliphaz when he was talking about the cunning of this demon. . . . It is barrenness of soul, not the darkness or the emptiness of places, which gives the demons power against us. And the providence of God sometimes allows this to happen so that we may learn from it.

Interestingly, St. John says that as we grow in the spiritual life, we will begin to detect the presence of spiritual beings through the presence or absence of fear.

The body is terrified by the presence of an invisible spirit. Yet when an angel stands nearby, the soul of the humble is exultant. So if we detect an angel by the effect he is producing, let us hasten to pray since our heavenly guardian has come to join us.

How do we overcome unmanly fears? The answer is clear: through sincere humility and heartfelt trust in God, and through the rejection of all satanic fantasies. Let us not allow fear to keep us from pursuing God. Let us look neither to the right nor to the left, but let us walk faithfully on that path which God has laid before us, looking unto Jesus, the Author and Finisher of our faith.

If your soul is unafraid even when the body is terrified, you are close to being healed.

Step 22

Humbling Ourselves

St. John labels Step 22, **On Vainglory.** His words of introduction are very enlightening:

> **As the occasion demands, let us talk about the unholy vice of self-esteem, the beginning and completion of the passions. . . . Like the sun which shines on all alike, vainglory beams on every occupation. What I mean is this. I fast, and I turn vainglorious. I stop fasting so that I will draw no attention to myself, and I become vainglorious over my prudence. I dress well or badly, and am vainglorious in either case. I talk or I hold my peace, and each time I am defeated. No matter how I shed this prickly thing, a spike remains to stand up against me.**

I am sure that each one of us can easily relate to what St. John is describing. Vainglory is the beginning of spiritual pride; it is the congratulation of self for work well

111

done. It is the desire for recognition from others, the love of praise. St. John writes:

> **The spirit of despair exults at the sight of mounting vice, the spirit of vainglory at the sight of the growing treasures of virtue.**

What are the signs that we have succumbed to this passion and been overwhelmed by this demon? St. John lists several. Vainglory enters our lives when we grow concerned about what other people think of us. It puts down its roots into our hearts when we begin to worry about their disapproval and to be pleased by their approval. It captures our hearts when we enjoy their words of praise. It takes over our hearts when we begin to work for these words of praise which bring us such joy. St. John writes:

> **A vainglorious man is a believer—and an idolater. Apparently honoring God, he actually is out to please not God but men. To be a showoff is to be vainglorious.**

> **Men of high spirit can endure offense nobly and willingly. But only the holy and the saintly can pass unscathed through praise.**

How can we conquer vainglory? St. John is very clear in his instructions.

> **The first step in overcoming vainglory is to remain silent and to accept dishonor gladly. The middle stage is to check every act of vainglory while it is still in thought. The end—insofar as one may talk of an end to an**

abyss—is to be able to accept humiliation before others without actually feeling it.

These words are so easy to type and to read—but not so easy to put into practice.

If there is one thing that we have been trained to do in our modern world, it is to sell ourselves, to get ourselves noticed, to push ourselves forward. We are taught from an early age to "dress for success." In school, we are given self-assertiveness training, and as we enter into high school, we take classes entitled, "How to sell yourself at your first job interview." As modern people, we are obsessed with our external appearance, controlled by the opinions of others, and overwhelmed by the need to fit in.

It is very easy for us to bring this attitude into the practice of our faith—to lose perspective and to begin to live our lives to please the crowd. This can cut two ways. Either it can motivate us to appear outwardly pious (i.e., saying the right things, reading the right books, making the right bows, attending the right services, keeping the right fasts, etc.) so that others will notice and say good things about us; or it can motivate us to back away from the full expression of our faith.

We are not always surrounded by people who are supportive of our faith. Sometimes, love for the praise and approval of men and fear that they will think we have become zealots can keep us from saying the right things, reading the right books, making the right bows, attending the right services, keeping the right fasts, etc. The key is our attitude! *Why* are we doing what we are doing?

How can we tell? One way to find out is to ask ourselves the following questions:

- Does my behavior change when no one else is around?
- Do I find myself telling others about all of my spiritual efforts and blessings?
- Do I believe my "press clippings"?
- Do I find myself replaying what others have said to me or what I have said to them over and over again in my mind?
- Do I act and talk as if I have experientially known spiritual truths that I have only read about?
- Do I become discouraged and quit when no one notices what I do and/or I do not receive the praise and thanksgiving I think I deserve?
- Do I hide my sins and failings from others, even to the point of lying or shading the truth so that my true faults are not discovered by others?
- Do I become defensive when I am criticized?
- Do I feel the need always to make sure that everyone knows why I did something?

If we answer "yes" to any of these, then the spirit of vainglory lives within us. Let us not be overly discouraged or depressed by this, but let us repent. As St. John notes:

It often happens that having been left naked by vainglory, we turn around and strip it ourselves more cleverly. For I have encountered some who embarked on the spiritual life out of vainglory, making therefore a bad start, and yet they finished up in a most admirable way because they changed their intentions.

How do we change our intentions? St. John's advice is very practical.

If ever we seek glory, if it comes our way uninvited, or if we plan some course of action because of vainglory, we should think of our mourning and of the blessed fear on us as we stood alone in prayer before God. If we do this we will assuredly outflank shameless vainglory, that is if our wish for true prayer is genuine. This may be insufficient. In which case let us briefly remember that we must die. Should this also prove ineffective, let us at least go in fear of the shame that always comes after honor, for assuredly he who exalts himself will be humbled not only there but here also. When those who praise us, or, rather, those who lead us astray, begin to exalt us, we should briefly remember the multitude of our sins and in this way we will discover that we do not deserve whatever is said or done in our honor.

I remember the words of one spiritual father to his son:

I am afraid that you will become proud. My fear for you comes from my deep love for you. For I know what happens to those who become proud. I know that God's love will seek to restore them and will motivate Him to save their souls. But I also know that the only means God can use to save a proud man is to humble him. This is good, but it is so painful. I want to spare you the pain of being humbled by God. Humble yourself, flee from pride and vainglory, so that God will exalt you rather than lower you.

I am also reminded of the words of two bishops I know. One says to his priests, "Don't praise me. It is very dangerous to praise a bishop or priest." The other says, each time I attempt to thank or praise him, "Thank God. Always, thank God." These holy men show us the way. Like St. John the Baptist, they always point people away from themselves, toward Christ.

It is very interesting that St. John of the Ladder insists the battle against pride is either won or lost on the ground of vainglory.

A worm, fully grown, often sprouts wings and can fly up high. Vainglory, fully grown, can give birth to pride, which is the beginning and the end of all evil.

What an insight into the spiritual life! I am so often overwhelmed by spiritual pride that I despair of ever being humble. To know that I can deal a fatal blow to my pride by working on my attachment to the praise of others brings me hope and encouragement. (Here the "fools for Christ" show us the way!)

To take baby steps: to stop talking about myself, to stop drawing attention to myself, to try to hide my labors and efforts, to stop needing to know what everyone is saying about me, to stop worrying about that one person who doesn't like me and the way I do things, to stop replaying that nice comment that someone made . . . This I understand. I haven't figured out how to do it all yet, but at least I know what I should be working on. The promise St. John holds out is enough to make me keep trying:

Anyone free of this sickness is close to salvation. Anyone affected by it is far removed from the glory of the saints.

Such, then, is the twenty-second step. The man untouched by vainglory will not tumble into the senseless pride which is so detestable to God.

Step 23

Beating Pride

Pride is a denial of God, an invention of the devil, contempt for men. It is the mother of condemnation, the offspring of praise, a sign of barrenness. It is a flight from God's help, the harbinger of madness, the author of downfall. It is the cause of diabolical possession, the source of anger, the gateway of hypocrisy. It is the fortress of demons, the custodian of sins, the source of hardheartedness. It is the denial of compassion, a bitter Pharisee, a cruel judge. It is the foe of God. It is the root of blasphemy.

With these words St. John introduces us to the twenty-third step of the Ladder: **On Pride.** And he makes it clear right from the beginning that we are dealing with a very serious spiritual ailment. How does spiritual pride develop? St. John says that it flows out of our love of the praise of men (vainglory). Its midpoint is **the shameless parading**

of our achievements, complacency, and unwillingness to be
found out. Its end is **the spurning of God's help, the exalting of
one's own efforts and a devilish disposition.** In words which are
frightening, St. John says:

> **A proud monk needs no demon. He has turned into one,
> an enemy to himself.**

A wise elder once said: "Think of a dozen shameful passions.
Love one of them, I mean pride, and it will take up the space of
all the other eleven."

Pride is a vice which destroys all virtue in our lives:

> **Pride loses the profits of all hard work and sweat.**

Pride closes the ears of God to our prayers:

> **They clamored but there was none to save them, because
> they clamored with pride. They clamored to God and
> He paid no heed.**

Ultimately, pride will take us to hell! St. John reminds us:

> **Pride and nothing else caused an angel to fall from
> heaven.**

How can we recognize that this spiritual ailment is afflicting
us? In a series of proverbs, St. John gives us several signs which
manifest its presence in our hearts:

- Spiritual pride manifests itself in a know-it-all, argumen-
  tative spirit:
  **A proud monk argues bitterly with others. The humble
  monk is loath to contradict them.**

- Spiritual pride manifests itself in a refusal to obey, a belief that we know better than our spiritual elders:
  The cypress tree does not bend to the ground in order to walk, nor does the haughty monk in order to gain obedience.
- Spiritual pride manifests itself in an aversion to correction, a belief that we are beyond the need for reproach and/or instruction:
  To reject criticism is to show pride, while to accept it is to show oneself free of this fetter.
- Spiritual pride manifests itself in a desire to lead and an innate belief that we know what needs to be done and how it needs to be done better than others:
  The proud man wants to be in charge of things. He would feel lost otherwise.
- Spiritual pride manifests itself in a false humility:
  An old man, experienced in these matters, once spiritually admonished a proud brother who said in his blindness, "Forgive me, father, but I am not proud." "My son," said the wise man, "what better proof of your pride could you have given than to claim that you were not proud?"
- Spiritual pride manifests itself in a lack of awareness of our own sins and shortcomings:
  Pride makes us forget our sins, for the remembrance of them leads to humility.
- Spiritual pride manifests itself in an inflated opinion of our own virtues:
  It happens, I do not know how, that most of the proud never really discover their true selves. They think they

have conquered their passions, and they find out how poor they really are only after they die.

- Spiritual pride manifests itself in thinking that we have already attained salvation, in forgetting the need to finish the race and the possibility of failure:
Do not be self-confident before judgment has been passed on you. Do not be stiff-necked, since you are a material being. Many although holy and unencumbered by a body were thrown out even from heaven.

How do we overcome pride in our lives? Once again, St. John's words are straight to the point. His advice can be summarized in the following points:

(1) Remember the example of the saints.

To overcome pride, it is helpful to keep always before us the struggles and virtues of the holy fathers and saints.

We should always be on the lookout to compare ourselves with the Fathers and the lights who have gone before us. If we do, we will discover that we have scarcely begun the ascetic life, that we have hardly kept our vows in a holy manner, and that our thinking is still rooted in the world.

It is so easy for us to compare ourselves with our contemporaries and think that we are doing pretty well. If we go to Vespers on Saturday night, how easy it is to notice who is not there! If we come to Matins on Sunday morning or attend weekday services, how easy it is for us to think that we are doing extra, superabundant labors for the Lord! In our day and age of easy Orthodoxy (what a priest friend of mine calls "Orthodoxy Lite"), it is a great temptation for those who are trying to live pious, traditional Orthodox lives to begin to think that they are somehow doing a lot for the Lord, that they are waging a serious and dedicated struggle and that they have achieved a level of spiritual maturity. One has only to look to the Fathers and saints to see how shallow and false this kind of thinking is.

- Do you think that you pray a lot?
  Remember St. Seraphim of Sarov, who prayed for a thousand days upon a rock, and be humbled.
- Do you think that your fasting is intense?
  Remember St. John of San Francisco, who ate but one meal a day and nothing at all during several weeks of Great Lent, and be humbled.
- Do you think that you have been consistent in your private prayers?
  Remember St. Herman of Alaska, who prayed the full monastic cycle of prayers by himself for over forty years on a deserted island in northern Alaska, and be humbled.
- Do you think that you have suffered for Christ?
  Remember the Forty Holy Martyrs of Sebaste, who sacrificed everything for Christ, and be humbled.
- Do you think that you have loved your enemies?
  Remember St. Elizabeth the Grand Duchess, who visited her husband's assassin and offered him her love and blessing, and be humbled.

Whatever you think you have done, there is a saint who reveals that what you have done is nothing. And not only this . . . anytime you are tempted to think that your labors for Christ are intense, remember the contemporary monks on Mount Athos and elsewhere who are struggling for your salvation, and be humbled.

(2) Remember your blessings.

To overcome pride, it is helpful for us to remember how many blessings we have received, *and* to remember that any advancements we have made in the spiritual life are directly a result of blessings which we did nothing to earn or to gain. St. John writes:

> **While it is disgraceful to be puffed up over the adornments of others, it is sheer lunacy to imagine that one has deserved the gifts of God. You may be proud only of the achievements you had before the time of your birth. But anything after that, indeed the birth itself, is a gift from God. You may claim only those virtues in you that are there independently of your mind, for your mind was bestowed on you by God. And you may claim only those victories you achieved independently of the body, for the body too is not yours but a work of God.**

(3) Remember that you owe everything to Christ.

To overcome pride, it is helpful to remember that everything we obtain by way of struggle in the spiritual life is offered to us only because of the struggle of Christ. No matter how hard we struggle, without Christ there would be no victory, because there would be no heaven. The doors of Hades would still be closed. The grave would still have its claim on us and we would be shut off from the presence of God. All of the gifts and graces, the visions and insights, the miracles and blessings which we experience in the context of our labors are only possible because of God's gracious Incarnation.

If we were to die ten thousand times for Christ, we would still not have repaid what we owe, for in value rather than in physical substance there is no comparison between the blood of God and that of His servants.

The struggle against pride is intense; for most of us, it will never end in this life. Let us embrace this struggle, knowing that if we are overcome by pride we will most certainly fail. We cannot avoid the struggle. It is necessary for our salvation.

Such is the twenty-third step. Whoever climbs it, if indeed anyone can, will certainly be strong.

STEP 24

LIVING MEEKLY

In this chapter, we turn our attention to Step 24 of the Ladder that leads to heaven: **On Meekness, Simplicity, Guilelessness, and Wickedness.** Having shown us the deep danger of pride, St. John wishes to lead us step by step to the virtue of humility (Step 25). Before we consider humility, however, he insists that we must consider meekness.

> The light of dawn comes before the sun, and meekness is the precursor of all humility. . . . Before gazing at the sun of humility we must let the light of meekness flow over us. If we do, we will then be able to look steadily at the sun. The true order of these virtues teaches us that we are totally unable to turn our eyes to the sun before we have first become accustomed to the light.

What is meekness? St. John answers:

Meekness is a mind consistent amid honor or dishonor. Meekness prays quietly and sincerely for a neighbor however troublesome he may be. Meekness is a rock looking out over the sea of anger which breaks the waves which come crashing on it and stays entirely unmoved. . . . Meekness works alongside of obedience, guides a religious community, checks frenzy, curbs anger.

We may define meekness further:

- A meek person is not quick to defend or justify himself in the presence and thoughts of others (see Num. 11).
- A meek person is not easily unsettled by the words and opinions of others.
- A meek person guards his heart carefully against the intrusion of thoughts of **frenzy** (i.e., against any thoughts which disturb his internal peace).
- A meek person is calm in the midst of disturbing events; he is not easily excited or provoked. He watches over his words, carefully choosing to utter only those which bring peace.
- A meek person does not project himself into conversations or situations in which his presence is not desired.
- A meek person does not jump in to correct everyone and everything.
- A meek person is willing to wait for God to act and does not believe that his action is necessary to God.
- A meek person knows how to pray and to be quiet.
- Most importantly, a meek person has no personal agenda: he is concerned only for God's will. And, in his meekness, he recognizes that often God's will unfolds itself in

ways that are unusual and unexpected. Thus, even in his concern for God's will, he is willing to wait calmly for God to accomplish His purpose. When he must act, he does so out of calm faith rather than panicky unbelief.

It is interesting that St. John connects meekness with simplicity and guilelessness:

A meek soul is a throne of simplicity, but a wrathful mind is a creature of evil.... Guilelessness is the joyful condition of an uncalculating soul.

This emphasis on simplicity and guilelessness is, of course, authentically Orthodox. One need only remember how often saints are praised for their simplicity to understand how fundamental this is to the Orthodox understanding of the heavenly ascent. St. John is very clear on its necessity:

Let us run from the precipice of hypocrisy, from the pit of duplicity.... People of this kind are fodder for demons.

What is simplicity? Without attempting to give a full definition (one must have it in order fully to explain it), let me try to draw a sketch of it. St. John uses three images as illustrations.

(1) Childhood
From childhood, we understand that simplicity is the absence of a concern to fit in. We all know that small children are oblivious to social realities and norms. If a young infant feels like screaming in the middle of the Divine Liturgy, she doesn't worry at all

that it might upset someone or break someone's idea of what should happen. She just screams. If she feels like going to the bathroom, she doesn't worry that others around might hear. She just goes. And she is not embarrassed if you take off her clothes and change her in the presence of other people. If she wants to eat, she doesn't care that it's not dinnertime. She doesn't change her behavior when she is around "important" people. If she is crabby, she's crabby everywhere with everyone. She loves for you to play with her, but she doesn't become angry and pout if you don't. She is always herself.

Those who have struggled to embrace simplicity live in much the same way. Fitting in with the crowd and compromising one's own integrity to do so are not part of the simple lifestyle. Certainly, those who are mature in their simplicity do not go around offending everyone all the time (unless they have been called by God to the extreme simplicity of holy foolishness). This is not the point. The point is that they are free from the necessity to change themselves, to become social or spiritual chameleons, in order to fit in and to meet the expectations of others.

(2) Adam in the Garden
From Adam in the Garden, we learn that simplicity is the absence of self-awareness. St. John writes:

> **As long as Adam had [simplicity], he saw neither the nakedness of his soul nor the indecency of his flesh.**

Adam was free from the desire to look in the mirror and the necessity to stand on the scale. This statement, if considered carefully, reveals to us a great deal about simplicity. Why do we look in the mirror? Why do we stand on the scale as often as we do?

Some of it is utilitarian (we have to look at least presentable if we are going to keep our jobs, etc.), but a great deal of it is vanity. Does not a lot of it spring from an unhealthy desire to see ourselves as other people see us? to find out how we look to others?

Here we see why St. John keeps mentioning hypocrisy as he discusses simplicity. Our outside appearance (very often including not only our clothes and hair, but also our actions) often becomes the equivalent of a mask, designed to keep people from seeing us as we really are. Our outside appearance thus becomes divorced from our inner self. The inherent, simple connection between our inner soul and outer body becomes distorted. This distortion wreaks havoc in our spiritual lives.

One major purpose of the spiritual disciplines is to bring stability and cohesion back into our soul-body relationship. I am reminded of the words spoken to describe St. John the Dwarf: "He is on the outside what he is on the inside." This is a tremendous definition of simplicity. I am also reminded of the testimony given by one college girl who had the opportunity to meet Fr. Seraphim Rose:

> I tried to prepare myself to meet him. When he walked in, he looked so different, with his long beard, long hair and long robe. I told myself that this was not really him, but just an external appearance, and that I had to see beyond it. I tried to separate the person from the outward appearance, since with so many people the latter has very little to do with the former. But with Fr. Seraphim I just couldn't do it. I found that what I saw was Fr. Seraphim; that is, his Orthodox faith, his monasticism, the black robe he wore as a symbol of repentance—this was part of

what he really was inside. They were inextricably bound together.

(3) St. Paul the Simple

From St. Paul the Simple, we learn that simplicity is linked to unquestioning obedience and firm faith. St. Paul was a disciple of St. Antony the Great, who joined the desert elder after catching his own wife in adultery. A hint of his simplicity may be seen even here, in an unsuspecting, trusting attitude towards others which him into trouble in the world, but won for him heavenly rewards.

St. Antony thought Paul too old to be a monk, but Paul submitted to the severest disciplines with such unquestioning obedience that in a relatively short time, he acquired spiritual powers even greater than St. Antony's. After relating his story, St. John of the Ladder draws this conclusion:

> **Fight to escape your own cleverness. If you do, then you will find salvation and an uprightness through Jesus Christ our Lord. Amen.**

I find the words of Fr. Seraphim Rose to be very enlightening on this subject:

> Accept simply the Faith you receive from your fathers. If there is a simple-hearted priest you happen to be in connection with, give thanks to God. Consider that, because you are so complex, intellectual and moody, you can learn a great deal from such simplicity. If we follow the simple path—distrusting our own wisdom, doing the best we can yet realizing that our mind, without warmth of heart, is a

very weak tool—then an Orthodox philosophy of life will begin to be formed in us (Monk Damascene Christensen, *Not of this World*, Fr. Seraphim Rose Foundation, Forestville, CA, 1993, p. 775).

St. John of the Ladder concludes:

If you have strength to take this step, do not lose heart. For now you are imitating Christ your Master and you have been saved.

STEP 25

DEVELOPING HUMILITY

St. John of the Ladder begins his discussion of the twenty-fifth step of the Ladder with these words:

Do you imagine that talk of such matters will mean anything to someone who has never experienced them? If you think so, then you will be like a man who with words and examples tries to convey the sweetness of honey to people who have never tasted it. He talks uselessly. Indeed I would say he is simply prattling.... Our theme sets before us as a touchstone a treasure stored safely in earthen vessels, that is, in our bodies. This treasure is of a quality that eludes adequate description. It carries an inscription of heavenly origin which is therefore incomprehensible so that anyone seeking words for it is faced with a great and endless task. The inscription reads as follows: "Holy Humility."

St. John's words are very important for us as we begin to discuss this important and most necessary step. There is something very misleading about reading about humility, as if one could learn about true humility from a book. In fact, St. John says this precisely:

> **Humility is a grace in the soul and with a name known only to those who have had experience of it. It is indescribable wealth, a name and a gift from God. "Learn from Me," He said; that is, not from an angel, not from a man, not from a book, but "from Me," that is, from My dwelling within you, from My illumination and action within you, for "I am gentle and meek of heart" (Matt. 11:29) in thought and in spirit, and your souls will find rest from conflicts and relief from evil thoughts.**

Humility is a virtue won through struggle. There is a very real sense in which humility can only be learned existentially, through the experience of the struggle for God. In the context of this struggle (which is inescapably a struggle for God, and thus, a struggle against oneself, the world, and most importantly, the devil), we are taught by God Himself what it means for us to be humble. Ultimately, we find that the greatest hindrance to humility is the stubborn pride of our own hearts.

Perhaps this is the first step towards learning how to be humble: to recognize in our hearts how proud we truly are. It is easy to know this intellectually, but intellectual knowledge is not sufficient for the attainment of true humility. It is our hearts that must become convinced of the depth of our pride and the absolute absence of true humility in our lives.

If we follow the counsel of the Fathers and begin to watch

carefully over our hearts, we will observe how truly proud we are. We will observe how our hearts warm when we are praised and how they become cold and calculating when we are criticized. We will observe how we cherish the memories of our successes and replay them over and over again. We will observe how much joy we find in ourselves. We will find deeply rooted anger over the mistreatment we have received from the hands of others. And when we attempt to change these things, we will find out how stubborn our hearts really are and how deeply pride has imbedded itself into the very fabric of our being.

Once again, this can only be learned through struggle. It is one thing to write about it and to give mental assent to it. But how many of us really *know* that this is true; how many of us *feel* that it is true; how many of us experience the torturous presence of pride from moment to moment? There is only way to learn: lifelong struggle with oneself.

The nature of this personal struggle is such that humility expresses itself in different ways in different people. Since humility is a grace of God in the soul, learned existentially in the context of my own individual struggle to find God, it is inescapably personal. What it means for me to be humble is tied to who I am, where I have come from, where I am going, and how I am supposed to get there. The uniqueness of my own road to God means that humility is going to be different for me than it is for anyone else. Furthermore, as I grow older and my life changes, humility will take on new meaning and new expressions. St. John puts it poetically:

The appearance of this sacred vine is one thing during the winter of passions, another in the springtime of

flowering, and still another in the harvesttime of all the virtues.

Having said all this, however, as beginners we are in need of some direction. No book can give us humility, nor can any book adequately describe what it will mean for us to be humble at all times in all places. But certainly there must be a beginner's manual. From the experience of those who have attained this virtue, there must be some time-tested advice. How can we recognize the presence of humility in our hearts? How can we water and fertilize this young plant when it begins to grow? What are its signs and what are its fruits?

St. John anticipates our questions and, in his wisdom, gives us general guidelines to follow in the specifics of our own struggle. Firstly, he reminds us that the struggle for humility is the most important struggle of our spiritual lives. Humility is victory over every passion:

> **The man with humility for his bride will be gentle, kind, inclined to compunction, sympathetic, calm in every situation, radiant, easy to get along with, inoffensive, alert and active. In a word, free from passion.**

> **If you wish to fight against some passion, take humility as your ally, for she will tread on the asp and the basilisk of sin and despair and she will tread under foot the lion and the serpent of physical devilishness and cunning (see Ps. 90:13).**

Humility is entrance into heaven:

Repentance lifts a man up. Mourning knocks at heaven's gates. Holy humility opens it.

Most importantly, humility is love of prayer:

You will know that you have this holy gift within you and not be led astray when you experience an abundance of unspeakable light together with an indescribable love of prayer.

Humility is the guardian of all other virtues:

Many have attained salvation without the aid of prophecies, illumination, signs and wonders. But without humility no one will enter the marriage chamber, for humility is guardian of such gifts. Without it, they will bring disaster on the frivolous.

Secondly, St. John teaches us how to recognize the presence of humility in our hearts. (Remember: his purpose in giving us these signs of humility is not to make us proud because they are there, but to make us humble because they are not!)

- The first sign of humility is:
  the delighted readiness of the soul to accept indignity, to receive it with open arms, to welcome it as something that relieves and cauterizes diseases of the soul and grievous sins.
  As the flip side of this, we are reminded:
  As soon as the cluster of holy humility begins to flower within us, we come, after hard work, to hate all earthly praise and glory.

- The second sign of humility is:
  the wiping out of anger—and modesty over the fact that it has subsided.
- The third sign of humility is:
  the honest distrust of one's own virtues, together with an unending desire to learn more.
  As the flip side of this, we are reminded:
  Holy humility has this to say: "The one who loves me will not condemn someone, or pass judgment on anyone, or lord it over anyone else, or show off his wisdom." Those of us who wish to gain understanding must never stop examining ourselves, and if in the perception of your soul you realize that your neighbor is superior to you in all respects, then the mercy of God is surely near at hand.

Thirdly, St. John teaches us how to cultivate the presence of humility in our hearts. Here he reminds us that there is not only one way to humility. The heights of humility may be scaled from various vantage points:

(1) Remembering our sins.

We can develop humility by reminding ourselves often of our sins. Nothing keeps us from thinking that we are holy like the remembrance of what we have done and are doing wrong.

> **Some drive out empty pride by thinking to the end of their lives of their past misdeeds, for which they were forgiven and which now serve as a spur to humility. . . . Others hold themselves in contempt when they think of their daily lapses.**

St. John tells the story of a holy monk who was tempted to think vainly. He wrote on the walls of his cell the names of all the virtues, and when he was tempted to think that he was a saint and a holy man, he went and stood before each name and remembered how many times he had failed to live out the virtue which was on his wall. True repentance leads to humility.

All are called to repent; this is the reason for the sacrament of confession. But not all are strong enough—psychologically, emotionally, or spiritually—to bear constant remembrance of past misdeeds. For some, this does not lead to humility, but to despair. Not all are capable of living such lives of constant remembrance. For these, St. John outlines another way to humility:

(2) Remembering God's grace.

We can develop humility by reminding ourselves of how much grace we have received.

> **Others, remembering the passion of Christ, think of themselves eternally in debt. . . . There are some—and I cannot say if they are to be found nowadays—who humble themselves in proportion to the gifts they receive from God and live with a sense of their unworthiness to have such wealth bestowed upon them, so that each day they think of themselves as sinking further into debt.**

If we cannot bear the constant remembrance of our sins, or if this grace has not been given to us, then perhaps we can humble ourselves by the constant remembrance of God's mercy and grace. This way is especially beneficial for those who have been specially gifted by God and/or who have lived reasonably pampered lives.

Never stop reminding yourself that where and who you are is very much a result of things completely beyond your control. Remind yourself of how different you would be if you had grown up with parents that didn't love you, if you had been sexually abused as a child, if you had serious learning disabilities, etc. Speak to your soul in this manner:

> *Isn't it true that much of what you pride yourself on has nothing to do with you? In fact, isn't it true that, with as many blessings and privileges as you have received, you should be a lot further along than you are? Haven't you squandered the blessings of God? Of what are you proud? What do you have that you did not receive? And if you did receive it, why do you boast as if you had not (1 Cor. 4:7)?*

True gratitude leads to humility.

But not all can walk this way. All, it is true, are called to be thankful. Each one of us must develop an attitude of gratitude, but for some (especially those who have struggled and experienced great pain) there are many things over which they are tempted to become bitter. Gratitude itself becomes a serious struggle. While they must engage in this struggle, there is another way that leads to humility.

(3) Remembering our weakness.

We can develop humility by reminding ourselves of how weak and vulnerable to sin we are.

Others come to possess this mother of graces by way of their continuous temptations, weaknesses and sins.

If we cannot continuously remind ourselves of our sin, and if we cannot remain continuously thankful, at least we should be able to remember at all times how easy it is for us to fall. After all, is there anyone who cannot remember falling into sin? Is there anyone among us who has not been taken in by Satan? Is there anyone who does not recall with embarrassment mistakes made in the past?

If we cannot find humility through repentance or through gratitude, let us embrace it through weakness. We are not strong in and of ourselves; we are vulnerable, we cannot defend ourselves spiritually or physically. Let us be humbled. This is why the Holy Fathers say that physical labor, vigils, fasting, etc. are important aids to humility. They reveal the weakness of our flesh, so that we might put no trust in it. Recognition of our own mortality and frailty leads to humility.

Someone discovered in his heart how beautiful humility is, and in his amazement he asked her to reveal her parent's name. Humility smiled, joyous and serene: "Why are you in such a rush to learn the name of my begetter? He has no name, nor will I reveal him to you until you have God for your possession. To Whom be glory forever." Amen.

The sea is the source of the fountain, and humility is the source of discernment.

STEP 26

DISCERNING GOD'S WILL FOR OUR LIVES

St. John of the Ladder introduces the twenty-sixth step thus:

> Among beginners, discernment is real self-knowledge; among those midway along the road to perfection, it is a spiritual capacity to distinguish unfailingly between what is truly good and what in nature is opposed to the good; among the perfect, it is a knowledge resulting from divine illumination, which with its lamp can light up what is dark in others. To put the matter generally, discernment is—and is recognized to be—a solid understanding of the will of God in all times, in all places, in all things; and it is found only among those who are pure in heart, in body, and in speech.

How many times do we struggle to know God's will for our lives? As St. John notes:

There are many roads to holiness—and to hell. A path wrong for one will suit another, yet what each is doing is pleasing to God.

How are we to live our lives? What are we to do? In a moment of crisis, when a decision has to be made and made quickly, what does God want us to do? What will please Him? What will bring us heavenly rewards? Am I hearing the voice of God or the voice of self—or, worse still, the voice of Satan? How do I know? Anyone who is traveling the spiritual road knows in the depths of his being how agonizing these questions truly are.

As the hart parched with thirst pants for running water (cf. Psalm 41:2), the monk longs for a knowledge or grasp of the good and divine will.

St. John speaks very practically in response to this longing. Out of his own tried and trusted experience, he offers advice for those who would know God's will. First, he insists:

Those who wish to discover the will of God must begin by mortifying their own will. Then, having prayed in faith and simplicity, all malice spent, they should turn humbly and in confidence to their fathers or even their brothers and they should accept their counsel as though from God Himself, even when that counsel goes against the grain, even when the advice comes from those who do not seem very spiritual.

St. John's words must be carefully examined in order to be

understood. He recognizes that it is easy for us to say that we want to know God's will when, in fact, we really only want our own will. It is also easy for us to convince ourselves that what God wants is what we want, and then to imagine that our voice is the voice of God. This deception (known as *prelest* in Slavonic) leads us to hell. Once we have confused our voice with God's, we are easy prey for the devil.

Humility, the recognition that our will is confused and confusing, is the necessary prelude to knowing the will of God. To keep us from playing games with ourselves, and to ensure that we are totally humbled before God so that we can be guided by Him, St. John suggests that we make no decisions without advice and agreement from others. Do nothing without a blessing! This blessing may be obtained from our father confessor, from the writings and examples of the saints, or from our spiritual brothers and sisters.

> **God, after all, is not unjust. He will not lead astray the souls who, trusting and guileless, yield in lowliness to the advice and decision of their neighbor. Even if those consulted are stupid, God immaterially and invisibly speaks through them and anyone who faithfully submits to this norm will be filled with humility.**

St. John also mentions other ways to develop humility and to gain discernment.

> **Some of those trying to discover the will of God abandoned every attachment.... They prayed hard for a fixed number of days and they laid aside any inclination of their souls, whether to do something or to resist it. In**

this way they figured out what God willed, either through some direct manner of intelligible communication from Him or by the complete evaporation from their souls of whatever it was they had proposed to do.

I personally have seen this work over and over again. We human beings are impulsive; our desires are awakened and immediately we want to fulfill them. Usually, if we say "no" to our immediate desires to do something, they fade away and are replaced by desires for other things. If we detach ourselves from that which awakened our desires, they tend to go away. This is especially true if we submit ourselves during this time to a strict regimen of prayer and fasting.

Human desires (even ones satanically inspired) cannot sustain themselves if they are detached from their objects and if they are not fed by constant thought and imagination. However, a call from God will grow stronger during a time of prayer and fasting. The will of God is not dependent upon human impulses. The more it is nurtured and fed with prayer and fasting, the stronger it grows. The more detached we are from those things which feed the flesh and its desires, *and* the more attached we are to those things which feed our soul, the more we are able to discern the will of God for our lives. In addition, those things which are of God last, whereas the things of our flesh fade.

I have experienced this myself many times. Sometimes I receive an inspiration to do something, to adopt an additional labor or struggle for God. My first step is to check it out with someone else, my father confessor and/or a spiritual brother and/or the spiritual writings of the Fathers, etc. Once it has been shown to be intrinsically good, I start doing it. If it is of God, I have found that it sticks, it becomes part of me. This does not mean that it is always easy, but the struggle is one which is part of who I am and how I am finding my own salvation. If it is not of God but of my own stupidity, this is quickly revealed.

St. John continues:

Others found so much trouble and distraction in whatever they were doing that they were led to think that bother of this sort could have come only from God, in accordance with the saying, "We wanted to come to you once and once again, but Satan prevented us" (1 Thess. 2:18).

How refreshing are these words, and how contrary to our normal way of thinking! We often start something which we think is of God, and as soon as it gets difficult we grow discouraged and think that maybe we made a mistake, maybe it really wasn't of God. How different is the reasoning of St. John! If we start something and experience tremendous troubles in the doing of it, then we are probably on the right track.

Satan will only oppose something that is good; the better and purer it is, the more Satan will try to stop us at every turn. Remember: Jonah found everything ready and in order for him when he was running away from God. The boat was in port and there was plenty of room.

However, lest we err in the opposite direction, St. John gives us another angle:

But there were others who found that venture of theirs had proved unexpectedly successful, and so they inferred that it had pleased God, and they went on to

declare that God helps everyone who chooses to do the right thing (cf. Rom 8:28).

To know God's will is not easy; we often make mistakes. This should keep us humble, but it should not depress us. St. John writes:

> God is not unjust. He will not slam the door against the man who humbly knocks. In everything we do, in what has to be done now or later, the objective must be sought from God Himself. And every act that is not the product of personal inclination or of impurity will be imputed to us for good, especially if it is done for the sake of God and not for someone else. This is so, even if the actions themselves are not completely good.

> An active soul is a provocation to demons, yet the greater our conflicts the greater our rewards. There will be no crown for the man who has never been under attack, and the man who perseveres in spite of any failures will be glorified as a champion by the angels.

> God judges us by our intentions, but because of His love for us He only demands from us such actions as lie within our power. Great is the man who does all that lies within his power, but greater still is the man who, in all humility, tries to do more.

> Our eyes are a light to all the body. Discernment of the virtues is a light to all the mind.

STEP 27

LEARNING HOW TO BE STILL

St. John begins his discussion of the twenty-seventh step in this way:

> **We are like purchased slaves, like servants under contract to the unholy passions. And because this is so, we know a little of their deceits, ways, impositions and wiles. We know of their evil despotism in our wretched souls. But there are others who fully understand the tricks of these spirits, and they do so because of the working of the Holy Spirit and because of the freedom they themselves have managed to achieve. We in our sickness can only imagine the sort of relief that would come with good health.**

These words remind me of those of St. Paul:

> *Eye has not seen, nor ear heard,*
> *Nor have entered into the heart of man*

The things which God has prepared for those who love Him
(1 Cor. 2:9).

St. John calls this relief **stillness.** Stillness may be equated to peace in the soul—the absence of spiritual warfare and the presence of calm.

It is interesting to note how St. John develops this theme. On the one hand, stillness is a reward that comes to the experienced spiritual warrior as a result of his many struggles. Those who are engaged in the beginning battles of the spiritual life are beset with many struggles. In their soul there is often much discord and strife. This is because the passions are rooted deep within the soul. When we descend into the heart in order to purify it, we find ourselves in intense hand-to-hand combat.

This combat often means that we live without peace. *There is no peace . . . for the wicked* (Is. 48:22). As long as there is wickedness within us, our peace will be less than complete. Peace becomes the goal, rather than the constant experience. We yearn for peace, we struggle for peace, we earnestly await the peace which comes from victory over our passions.

Of course, it is paradoxical to say that we must struggle for peace. Peace, in its most ideal expression, is the absence of struggle. Those who are advanced in the spiritual life often obtain this state:

The final point is when one has no longer a fear of noisy disturbance, when one is immune to it. He who when he goes out does not go out in his intellect is gentle and wholly a house of love, rarely moved to speech and never to anger.

We beginners in the spiritual life cannot imagine what it would be like to be totally unaffected by the disquietude of the world; it is beyond our ability to comprehend never being tempted to speak in haste and never experiencing the movements of anger in our hearts. The beginner must be content with experiencing moments of this peace. He must strive to win this peace by overcoming all the passions which seek to overthrow it. Here is where the struggle for peace begins. We cannot achieve this level of peace unless we are willing to embrace the struggle for it:

He who has achieved stillness has arrived at the very center of the mysteries, but he would never have reached these depths if he had not first seen and heard the sound of the waves and of the evil spirits.

When we first embrace the spiritual life, we are unaware of how little peace there is in our souls. Most people don't even think about the state of their souls, let alone whether they are peaceful. This is not to say that they experience peace. They don't. Any look at the mad frenzy of activity in our modern world immediately convinces us of the lack of peace which is found there. But we are surrounded with so much relentless noise and unceasing activity that we seldom stop to realize that the absence of peace in the world stems from the peaceless state of our souls. It is only when we begin to center our thoughts on the spiritual world within by pushing far from us the noise of the external world that we notice how little peace is found there.

The first notice of this peacelessness is enough to drive many back to the diversions of the world. For some, the existential pain of their passionate soul is too great to bear, and they choose to run away rather than stay and face it. For those who choose to stay, the experience of the true state of their souls is a necessary lesson. We first learn the presence of our soul by its pain rather than its peace. As we continue to grow in our spiritual lives, it is this pain which will always direct us back to the concerns of the soul when we begin to stray.

As we set a priority on peace, we will begin to notice more and more the things in our lives that rob us of peace. We will begin to find the noise of this world to be a hindrance rather than a help. We will notice how much of our time is spent following distractions. We will begin to change our lifestyles on the basis of what produces peace in our souls. We will inevitably be led to a love of quiet and solitude. St. John notes:

> **The solitary runs away from everyone, but does so without hatred . . . The solitary does not wish to be cut off from the divine sweetness.**

This does not mean that pursuit of peace will necessarily make us all hermits who despise social interaction with people. What it does mean is that we will pursue relationships which enhance our peace; we will build our relationships on those activities which feed the soul rather than the passions. In this way, the struggle for peace becomes a struggle to let go—a struggle to find and pursue the one thing which alone is needful.

> **He who has truly attained stillness ignores the flesh. God does not make false promises.**

The important thing to note is that this is a gradual process. St. John is very quick to point out the dangers of embracing too much stillness before we are spiritually ready:

The man who is foul-tempered and conceited, hypocritical and a nurse of grievances, ought never to enter the life of solitude, for fear that he should gain nothing but the loss of his sanity.

As with so many other steps of the Ladder, St. John does not want to produce a bunch of spiritual copycats who embrace certain labors because others have embraced them. St. John is concerned that we act in a way that is authentically part of our own personal ascent to heaven. What is important is that we undertake any **holy way of life because of a delight in, a thirst for the love and sweetness of God.**

As we noted in previous chapters, this is not to be done without the advice and counsel of our father confessor and spiritual brothers. But having obtained this counsel, we must then pursue the peace which God alone can bring. As we pursue this peace, the path we are to walk to heaven will be made clear to us. We will judge any activity on the basis of its effect on our souls: Does it produce peace or does it reawaken the pain of a divided soul? This, at least in part, is what the Prophet David advises when he writes, *Seek peace and pursue it* (Ps. 34:14).

Above all, we must remember that the path to internal peace is not an easy one. Therefore, we must prepare ourselves for a long struggle.

Take hold of the walking stick of patience, and the dogs will soon stop their impudent harassment. Patience is a labor that does not crush the soul. It never wavers under interruptions, good or bad. The patient soul is a faultless worker who has turned his faults into

**victories. Patience sets a boundary to the daily on-
slaught of suffering. It makes no excuses and ignores
the self.**

We will not achieve the state of constant peace in a day. Perhaps it is enough for us today not to have allowed anger to enter
our soul; perhaps it is enough for us to have refrained from that
idle word which stirs up passion; perhaps it is enough for us to
have refrained from viewing that which would have aroused our
sexual passions. Each day we add virtue to virtue. Each day we
embrace the struggle. Each day we repent of our failures. Each
day we continue the struggle. In this way, although we may never
be completely successful, we will never stop trying. And God
who grants the prize will consider our struggles to be victory and
will grant us His peace for eternity.

**Blessed is he who hopes; thrice blessed is he who lives
to see the promise of being an angel.**

STEP 28

SEEKING UNION WITH GOD THROUGH PRAYER

St. John introduces Step 28 with these words:

Prayer is by nature a dialog and a union of man with God. Its effect is to hold the world together. It achieves a reconciliation with God.

As we noted in the beginning of our study of the Ladder, the goal of all spiritual labors is communion with God. We do not seek an abstract vision of the Divine, nor do we labor for a legal verdict declaring us "not guilty." Rather, we aim at communion and union: we set our sights on the true, intimate knowledge of God which is eternal life (see John 17:3). According to St. John Climacus, prayer must be looked at as both the means to and the achievement of this knowledge.

The goal of prayer is *God*. This is important to note as we begin. In prayer and through prayer we seek Him.

How easy it is for us to reduce prayer to the fulfillment of some external rule of prayer which must be completed before we can continue on with the fulfillment of our other external requirements. The great tragedy of our spiritual lives is that prayer itself can become part of this world and its ways, rather than an abandonment of this world so as to pursue the next.

> **Rise from love of the world and love of pleasure. Put care aside, strip your mind, refuse your body. Prayer, after all, is a turning away from the world, visible and invisible. What have I in heaven? Nothing. What have I longed for on earth besides You? Nothing except simply to cling always to You in undistracted prayer. Wealth pleases some, glory others, possessions others, but what I want is to cling to God and to put the hopes of my dispassion in Him (cf. Ps 72:25, 28).**

Understood in this light, prayer is itself a means of purification and of judgment.

> **War reveals the love of a soldier for his king, and the time and practice of prayer show up a monk's love for God. So your prayer shows where you stand.**

Prayer is a mirror, showing to us the true nature of our desires and of our love. If we love God, we will love to pray. The stronger the love for God, the more our hearts will be drawn to the dialogue of prayer, the more He will be the object of our thoughts and desires, the more He will consume us and become the end of our struggles.

Prayer has its external aspects: the words, the rule, the prostrations, the knots on the rope. But these external aspects must find their realization in the internal state of our soul. St. John outlines a continuous method of prayer which incorporates both of these:

Get ready for your set time of prayer by unceasing prayer in your soul.

For the true struggler for God, prayer is not episodic; it is a way of life. Its external expression changes: sometimes it is the reading of psalms, other times the singing of Church hymns; still further, it may be the quiet saying of the Jesus prayer or the recollection of God in the fulfillment of our daily tasks. Gradually, prayer establishes its own rhythm in our lives. In the beginning we force ourselves to pray; in the end it is prayer itself which forces us.

For those who are beginning in the spiritual life, prayer requires hard work.

Make the effort to raise up, or rather, to enclose your mind within the words of your prayer; and if, like a child, it gets tired and falters, raise it up again. The mind, after all, is naturally unstable, but the God Who can do everything can also give it firm endurance.

Here the external aspects of prayer dominate:

Because of our imperfection we need quantity as well as quality in the words of our prayer, the former making a way for the latter.

We can only learn to pray one way: by doing it. And by doing lots of it . . . over and over again, training our hearts to recognize and feel the words spoken by our mouths and considered in our brains.

Until we have acquired true prayer, we are like those who introduce children to walking.

I remember when my daughter first learned to walk. As I watched her learn, I was amazed at how she practiced walking by going around and around the same table. Some days she did nothing but walk: sometimes holding things in her hands, sometimes not, but always walking, walking, walking. In this way, walking is internalized—through the external discipline of repetition, walking became part of her.

St. John says that the same thing occurs in the spiritual life. In the beginning we go around and around the same table. We say the same prayers over and over again. We force ourselves to practice. Very often this seems strange and foreign to us. It does not seem natural; we totter and stumble. We finish our prayers and feel as if we have simply said words without really praying them. We may often feel hypocritical in our prayers, as if they are external and thus "fake." This is the beginning of prayer. If we persevere, pushing ourselves to say the words and urging our hearts to join the mind and the mouth, prayer will become internalized.

St. John puts it this way:

If the servants of praise are not sharing our company, we may openly put on the appearance of those at prayer. For among the weak, the mind often conforms to the body.

Prayer will not be something which comes from the outside, but it will come from the inside out. The words will flow from our hearts, rather than off the page. We will still say and think the same words (just as my daughter will always walk by putting one foot in front of the other), but these words will be ours, rather than someone else's. Our mouths, minds and hearts will be one. Our being will be united in prayer. This is the middle stage of prayer.

We must persevere in our prayer, not allowing our hearts to become distracted by passion and/or sensual pleasure. St. John notes:

> **Prayer is tarnished when we stand before God, our minds seething with irrelevancies. It disappears when we are led into useless cares. It is robbed when our thoughts stray without our realization of the fact. And it is defiled when we are in any way under attack.**

If we persevere, the experience of prayer becomes so much a part of us that the words themselves fade away and prayer becomes ecstasy and the immediate presence of God. This is the third and final stage: this is deification, the heights of theosis, to which only the saints attain in this life.

As we struggle to pray, there are several attitudes which we must be careful to maintain. The first is humility:

> **However pure you may be, do not be forward in your dealings with God. Approach Him rather in all humility and you will be given still more boldness.**

Satan tries to rob us of our humility during prayer by taking away from us the simplicity necessary to true prayer. He divides us by

getting us to think about ourselves even as we are praying. We
observe ourselves from the outside, thinking about how well we
are praying, how long we have been praying, etc. (How often
does this happen during the Divine Liturgy, when we think about
how we are sounding to others!) It is not only what we observe
which is the problem; it is the act of observation itself. To pray is
to lose ourselves in God; it is to abandon the pursuit of self by
pursuing God.

> **The hour of prayer is no time for thinking over necessities, not even spiritual tasks, because you may lose the better part (cf. Luke 10:42).**

Satan also tries to rob us of our humility after we pray by
telling us how good we are and how effective and powerful our
prayers are for others. Once again, notice how he tempts us to
externalize our prayer and to focus not on God (who is the
essence of true prayer) but on ourselves as "pray-ers." The truth
is, we cannot pursue God so long as we think about ourselves.
St. John is absolutely insistent that we not fall into this trap:

> **Do not become conceited when you have prayed for others and have been heard, for it is their faith which has been active and efficacious.**

Another important attitude necessary for true prayer is gratitude. St. John advises:

> **Heartfelt thanksgiving should have first place in our book of prayer.**

As is revealed by and in the Divine Liturgy, the height of
true prayer is Eucharist (thanksgiving). This is why the Divine

Liturgy is the central prayer of the Christian. All prayer, to be true prayer, must be eucharistic. This certainly means prayer must flow out of a thankful heart. Before it becomes intercession, prayer is first a response to grace received. A thankful heart is of necessity driven to give thanks. It cannot remain silent, but it must communicate its thankfulness to the Source of blessings.

It is this drive for communication which also links our own prayer to that of others. Thankful hearts are driven to declare their thankfulness to others. The Psalmist exclaims:

I will declare Your name . . . in the midst of the assembly (Ps. 22:22).

Union with others takes place most truly in the context of shared thanksgiving.

Here we see the power of the Eucharist and the importance of the eucharistic community. The Divine Liturgy is union with God and with all of creation. In the Divine Liturgy all that is created, with one voice and one priestly action, offers to God thanksgiving for all that God has done for us. At the head of this thanksgiving, as both its expression and its expresser, is the High Priest, Jesus Christ Himself.

For thou thyself art He that offers and is offered, that accepts and is distributed, O Christ our God, and unto thee we ascribe glory, together with thy Father who is from everlasting and thine all-holy, good and life-giving Spirit, now and ever and unto ages of ages (priest's prayer before the Great Entrance, St. John Chrysostom's Liturgy).

So important is this eucharistic connection that St. John can write:

Our good Redeemer, by speedily granting what is asked, draws to His love those who are grateful. But He keeps ungrateful souls praying a long time before Him, hungering and thirsting for what they want, since a badly trained dog rushes off as soon as it is given bread and leaves the giver behind.

Still further, for our prayer to lead to union with God, it is always necessary for it to be offered in a spirit of contrition. St. John notes:

Even if you have climbed the whole ladder of the virtues, pray still for the forgiveness of sins. Heed Paul's cry regarding sinners "of whom I am first" (1 Tim. 1:15).

In another place he writes:

Total contrition is necessary for everyone.

If we ever appear in God's presence and think that we belong there, if we ever lose sight of the priority of grace and our need for it at all times, then we have lost prayer. It is certain that we are not talking to God, but only to ourselves—or (worse yet) to Satan, who has the capacity to transform himself into an angel of light. Contrition is the key to being delivered from spiritual delusion. Those who pray in a spirit of repentance are not easily fooled by Satan and his demonic hosts, for:

. . . these unholy beings are afraid that you may earn a crown as a result of your battle against them through prayer, and besides, when scourged by prayer they will run away as though from a fire.

Some time ago I was invited to a "prayer breakfast" sponsored by some conservative Christian politicians. At this breakfast, many speakers talked about religious subjects, and around each table there was much discussion. At the end, I was invited to give the benediction. Before I prayed, I prefaced my prayer with the remark that it is ironic that at most "prayer breakfasts" we spend the majority of time talking among ourselves. St. John ends his comments with a similar statement:

You cannot learn to see just because someone tells you to do so. For that, you require your own natural power of sight. In the same way, you cannot discover from the teaching of others the beauty of prayer. Prayer has its own special teacher in God, who "teaches man knowledge" (Ps. 93:10). He grants the prayer of him who prays. And He blesses the years of the just.

STEP 29

GROWING BEYOND OUR PASSIONS

As we approach our consideration of Step 29, I am reminded of the story of St. Arsenius the Great, who once was asked by his disciples if there was anything more to the spiritual life than they were experiencing. Apparently, they thought that they had somehow made it to the heights and were secretly priding themselves on their advanced spirituality. St. Arsenius said, "Only this . . ." And with that, he held his hand up and his fingers became beams of light.

In Step 29, this is essentially what St. John Climacus does for us. He shows us the heights of spirituality, the exalted state of **Dispassion.** Listen to his description:

By dispassion I mean a heaven of the mind within the heart, which regards the artifice of the demons as a contemptible joke. A man is truly dispassionate—and is known to be such—when he has cleansed his flesh of all corruption; when

he has lifted his mind above everything created, and has made it master of all the senses; when he keeps his soul continually in the presence of the Lord and reaches out beyond the borderline of strength to Him. And there are some who would claim that dispassion is resurrection of the soul prior to that of the body, while others would insist that it is a perfect knowledge of God, a knowledge second only to that of the angels.

Dispassion is an uncompleted perfection of the perfect.... After entering this heavenly harbor, a man, for most of his earthly life, is enraptured, like someone already in heaven, and he is lifted up to the contemplation of God....

The man deemed worthy to be of this sort during his lifetime has God always within him, to guide him in all he has to say or do or think. The will of the Lord becomes for him a sort of inner voice through illumination. All human teaching is beneath him.

If we look at these descriptions, we have to admit that they are pretty amazing. It is hard for me to imagine being cleansed of all corruption; it is equally difficult for me to imagine being beyond the temptations of the flesh. It is truly beyond my ability to comprehend being a master of my senses. I consider it a good day if I have not given in to my senses; if I have restrained them. It is a spiritually successful day if I have, for example, held my tongue when provoked by my children's misbehavior. My whole life is spent dealing with my passions and trying to restrain them. What St. John is describing is quite different. He is talking about a spiritual state where the passions no longer exist!

Why does he lay this out before us? For at least two reasons: (1) to keep us from spiritual pride, and (2) to motivate us to spiritual labor. It is easy for us to become complacent in our spiritual life, to be satisfied with what we have achieved and to lose the impetus to pursue more. This, of course, is a satanic ploy, for the reality is that once we have stopped pursuing God we begin to lose what we have already gained. If we are not going forward in our spiritual lives, it is certain that we are going backwards. It is equally easy for us falsely to assume that we are at the heights of spiritual endeavor when we are yet at its beginning.

In this chapter, it is as if St. John is standing before us and proclaiming: "There is more! There is more! There is more!" It is as if he is beckoning to us to follow him, in the words of Reepicheep from *The Chronicles of Narnia:* "Further up and further in!" Listen to St. John's words:

> **O my brothers, we should run to enter the bridal chamber of this palace, and if some burden of past habits or the passage of time should impede us, what a disaster for us!**

In another place he says:

> **Brothers, let us commit ourselves to this, for our names are on the lists of the devout. There must be no talk of "a lapse," "there is no time," or "a burden." To everyone who has received the Lord in baptism, "He has given the power to become children of God" (John 1:12).**

In my observations of myself, I have noticed a sinful tendency to be satisfied with something less than dispassion. I grow weary of the struggle and I long to "be there" already. In my laziness I then lower the goal. I reduce holiness to a set of external rules; to a repeatable pattern of external behaviors.

Once I have lowered the goal, I don't have to struggle as much. Once I have equated holiness with external correctness, I can feel good about myself. I can be "holy" and feel good about myself at the same time. "I am right!" "I am correct." "I am keeping the canons." "I have not broken my fast." "I say my rule of prayer."

Soon I begin to see myself as an authentic spiritual guide for others. I begin to compare myself constantly with others and can even fancy myself to be a reliable judge of their holiness. Without being aware of it, I have fallen into *prelest*, spiritual delusion.

St. John's words in this chapter are a wake-up call. Much like St. Arsenius' beaming fingers, they remind me of how far I am from spiritual perfection. They humble me. But they also motivate me. They set the goal before me and promise me that through my struggles, my attempts to deal with my own sin and controlling passions, by the grace of God, I am inch by inch, step by step, making it. The goal is high: dispassion leading to illumination.

The height of the goal reaffirms the necessity of struggle. Nothing in this life comes easily. The more important it is, the more work it requires. These are facts of life. Thus, in my spiritual life, when I am tempted to despair, to quit, to accept second best, to abandon the struggle, I remind myself of just how wonderful the prize is. St. John says:

Think of dispassion as a kind of celestial palace, a palace of the King of heaven.

I know that is where I want to live. Getting there won't be easy; it will require much work, struggle, and pain; but the promise reassures me that it is worth all of that. A small hut may be easier to attain, but it is not where I want to live. I have my eyes set on a mansion, a celestial palace wherein dwell the King and all of his attendants.

Is there more?

Blessed dispassion raises the poor mind from earth to heaven, raises the beggar from the dunghill of passion. And love, all praise to it, makes him sit with princes, that is with holy angels, and with the princes of God's people.

Step 30

Achieving the Heights of the Virtues

We come to the end of our study of *The Ladder of Divine Ascent:* the thirtieth step. St. John introduces it in this way:

> And now at last, after all that has been said, there remains that triad, faith, hope and love, binding and securing the union of all. "But the greatest of these is love" (1 Cor. 13:13), since that is the very name of God Himself.

As we remarked in the very beginning of our study, the Ladder of Divine Ascent is a way to union with God. This is the goal of the spiritual life: direct, unhindered, and undistracted communion with the Holy Trinity. Everything that St. John has outlined, the negative and the positive, has been presented with this goal in mind: to prepare us to know God and, in knowing God, to experience life eternal.

What is the highest pinnacle of the knowledge of God? When is our labor no longer preparation for, but actual enjoyment of the presence of God? St. John answers: **when we love.** He writes:

> **Love, by its nature, is a resemblance to God, insofar as this is humanly possible. In its activity it is inebriation of the soul.**

In another paragraph he explains:

> **Not even a mother clings to her nursing child as a son of love clings to the Lord at all times.**

In still another place, he writes:

> **Love grants prophecy, miracles. It is an abyss of illumination, a fountain of fire, bubbling up to inflame the thirsty soul. It is the condition of angels, and the progress of eternity.**

It is truly significant that St. John isolates love as the highest expression of spirituality. Those of us who have grown up in the West have tended to associate great spiritual progress with either intellectual achievement or social action. These are not antithetical to the spiritual life, but neither do they represent its highest attainment. The person who truly knows God is love, even as God is love.

This too is an important consideration. We all, from time to time, love. Love is something we do and something we give. At best, love is an attribute which is part of our inner selves. In this respect, for us, love is most often premeditated. We think and plan to love. This is the beginning of the spiritual life.

Those fully deified do not *practice* love as an expression of forethought or will, but they themselves have *become* love. Here is where true union with God takes place. To know the heart of God is to know love. Love is not an attribute of God which takes its place among the other attributes of God. Love *is* God, and God is love.

Everything He does, even His punishment and wrath against sin, is an expression of His love. To love is to be obsessed with the thing or person which is loved. The deified ones are completely overtaken by desire for God Himself. St. John explains:

> **Someone truly in love keeps before his mind's eye the face of the beloved and embraces it there tenderly. Even during sleep the longing continues unappeased, and he murmurs to his beloved. That is how it is for the body. And that is how it is for the spirit. A man wounded by love had this to say about himself—and it really amazes me—"I sleep (because nature commands this) but my heart is awake (because of the abundance of my love)" (Song of Songs 5:2). You should take note, my brother, that the stag, which is the soul, destroys reptiles and then, inflamed by love, as if struck by an arrow, it longs and grows faint for the love of God (cf. Ps 41:1).**

This kind of consuming and exhilarating love for God is a gift, a grace, which comes from Him. This is the mystical side of the spiritual life. We can prepare ourselves to receive God's love; this is the ascetical side. But true love comes from God and draws us back to God. Having ascended the Ladder through the practice of the virtues, at its pinnacle we encounter the Eternal

Mystery. We are drawn into that Light which is also Darkness and that Darkness which is also Light, and we learn the meaning of the saying:

We love Him because He first loved us (1 John 4:19).

We encounter Someone bigger, more powerful, and more real than all of our feeble attempts to understand Him. We find the End of our search, and in experiencing Him, realize the End to be only the Beginning.

This is our hope: to know even as we are known and to love even as we are loved. It is this hope which must fuel all of our labors and ascetic striving. Our works will not save us; no Orthodox Christian believes they could. Our works merely prepare us to be saved. No one will be saved without preparation, but no one's preparation is salvific in the ultimate sense of the word. To be saved, to be deified, is to experience *love* in its fullest and purest expression.

What is it that every human being desires in the depths of his soul? What motivates and prompts the vast energies of humanity? Is it not the search for love? On the other hand, what is it that lies behind the savage, vicious destruction of humanity by humanity? Is it not the abandonment of love, the mistaken substitution of lust for love, and/or the loss of hope in the existence of love?

God is Love! Until we make the connection, we will live tragically misguided and misguiding lives. Our lives will be empty, counterfeit, destructive expressions of what might and should have been. "Looking for love in all the wrong places," entrapped by our dedication to the pursuit of sensual pleasure, we proceed from preoccupation with lust to preoccupation with death. We continually lower ourselves and become in action and thought more and more base. Restless in soul, abused and tormented by our lack of love, we, in turn, become abusers and tormentors of others. Well did Blessed Augustine say, "Our souls are restless until they find their rest in Thee."

Why? Because our souls can only rest in true Love, and it is God alone who loves mankind. That is why those who have scaled these heights, in looking back upon the rest of humanity, always weep. They weep as Jesus wept, looking upon the city of Jerusalem:

> *How often I wanted to gather your children together, as a hen gathers her brood under her wings, but you were not willing! (Matt. 23:37; Luke 13:34).*

At the end of his discussion, St. John records for us the teaching of Love Himself:

My love, you will never be able to know how beautiful I am unless you get away from the grossness of the flesh. So let this ladder teach you the spiritual union of the virtues. And I am there on the summit, for as the great man said, a man who knew me well: "Remaining now are faith, hope, and love, these three. But love is the greatest of them all" (1 Cor. 13:13).

ALSO BY FATHER JOHN MACK . . .

Preserve Them, O Lord

A guide for Orthodox couples in developing marital unity:
- premarital counseling for engaged couples;
- marriage enrichment for those who are already married;
- the development of an Orthodox understanding of marriage for those new to the Orthodox Faith.

Preserve Them, O Lord is the resource you need. It gives you insightful guidance from an experienced pastoral counselor, supplemented by:
- workbook exercises that help you understand yourself and your partner;
- over 70 pages of supplemental readings on topics both spiritual and practical;
- quotes from Scripture, the Fathers, and the wedding liturgy illuminating the patristic view of love, sex, and marriage.

paperback / 214 pages / ISBN 1-888212-01-2
Order No. 002012
$12.95 plus applicable tax, shipping and handling

For further ordering information, or to request a catalog of Conciliar's other books, booklets, brochures, and gift items, please contact Conciliar Press at (800) 967-7377 or (831) 336-5118, or visit our website at www.conciliarpress.com.